Disturbed by Joy

Disturbed by Joy

Sermons

by

Edmund A. Steimle

FORTRESS PRESS · PHILADELPHIA

To

SONDRA, LINDA, AND CHIP

Preface

The sermons in this volume have had checkered careers. All of them have been presented on radio over the Protestant Hour Network and most of them have also been preached in school, college, and seminary chapels, in parish churches, and in assemblies of churchmen. A minimum of editing has been done in order to preserve so far as possible the essentially oral quality of preaching, for sermons are meant to be heard rather than read. They are offered here at the prompting of a number of friends to whom I express my debt. I am also grateful to Mrs. Elsa B. Williams for the arduous task of preparing the typescript. The book is dedicated to my children who have done their part in keeping me close to reality. Where the sermons lose touch with the world around us and within us, the fault is mine not theirs.

EDMUND A. STEIMLE

Greensboro, Vermont
August, 1966

Contents

PART I

"Art thou he that should come?"

Between the Times

One of the recurring signs along the highways, mixed in with advertisements for motels, gasoline, and beer, is this incongruous announcement, "Jesus is coming soon." What can it possibly mean? I often wonder how they picture it: That an apparition will appear in the sky? That Jesus will appear incognito on the earth in the form of some strange teacher? That the whole world is going up in smoke, the whole business engulfed in one vast mushroom cloud? That we're going to die and meet Jesus at the moment of death? I've often wondered just how these people who put up the signs picture it: "Jesus is coming soon."

I'm sure of one thing, however. Those outside the churches haven't the foggiest notion of what it means and I suspect a good many churchgoers are equally confused. And yet millions of Christians all over the world repeat Sunday after Sunday, not only: "I believe in Jesus Christ, born, died, rose again . . ." but also this: "From thence he shall come to judge both the quick and the dead." And this is not simply a phrase in the Creed, for the Creed here reflects any number of passages in Scripture which speak of the end of the age and of Christ coming again. What shall we do with it? As the King of Siam would have put it, "It's a puzzlement!"

Well, first of all, let's look at the fact that every year the church, both Catholic and Protestant, sets apart these four weeks before Christmas as the Advent season. A preparation for Christmas, of course, but always more than that. The clear implication is that as at the first Advent Christ came to earth in Bethlehem, so in the second Advent he will come again. One of the most treasured Christmas carols, "O Come, O Come Emmanuel . . ." reflects the same double theme.

Of course, we have domesticated the carol and the whole Advent season, for that matter, and made of it simply a preparation for the day. But then when the day comes, there is an inevitable anticlimax. Except for the very young, Christmas Day never quite lives up to its advance billing. There is no "peace on earth" brought by the Christ child, at least no more than there was before; and no more "good will to men" than before—perhaps less, since there has been more thought for others before Christmas than on the day itself. And so, because Christ was born in times past, we look forward to his "coming again" on Christmas, but when the day arrives, nothing happens! It's been a pleasant little pageant in which we all play some token part and little more.

Is then this domestication of Advent the last best word on the matter? We live in the afterglow of a great event, the coming of Christ to earth two thousand years ago; but there is nothing comparable to it in the future. Is that it? Except for a wistful kind of birthday celebration each year on December 25? Or is there a hint of something more in the undercurrent of excitement which creeps into these days before Christmas despite the inevitable anticlimax;

when we live, as it were, "between the times," between an event in the past and an event in the future both of which shed a glow over the days between?

We probe here into the mystery of time itself. And it is a baffling mystery. As Augustine put it, "I know what time is until someone asks me." You know perfectly well what I mean when I say, "now." But no one has ever been able to define satisfactorily what "now" actually means. We say it is a moving line between the past and the future, yet as soon as you try to put your finger on the line, in that very act the present has already become past. Perhaps the best we can say is that "now" is living between the times. As George Buttrick puts it, "The man you are at any present moment is the fashioning of all your yesterdays—their hopes, joys, fears, failures, and prayers. But the present moment is also the anticipation of the future immediate or distant . . . freighted with longings and resolves."[1] We live—and the only time we live—is in this present "now," a time between the times.

Moreover, the significance of the present "now" depends both upon the vivid significance of the past and the vivid significance of the future. If I am left with time on my hands or if time hangs heavy—in short, if I am bored now—it is simply another way of saying that there is nothing much in the past or the future which intrigues me.

Nor are there any halfway measures here. If the past alone is significant for me but the future looks drab or hopeless, then my present becomes a feeding on the past,

[1] George A. Buttrick, "No Time Like the Present," a sermon preached in May, 1949, and published in *The Madison Avenue Church News*, Vol. XI, No. 7 (October, 1949).

living on memories, and before long I'll be trotting off to the nearest psychiatrist. If, on the other hand, the future alone is significant for me and the past is drab or nightmarish, then the "now" is equally unbearable and I project myself into the future in excessive daydreams or in suicide. I wonder, for example, if it would not be more accurate for the suicide to say, I can't face the endless repetition of the past, rather than, I can't face the future. His choice of death means that that future is more desirable than any other, especially if it means oblivion.

But there are moments when time doesn't hang heavy, it flies! And always because both the past *and* the future are significant. If you're reading a book and you can't put the book down *now,* it's because what you have already read leads you to look forward so eagerly to what is coming next that the present "now" is all-absorbing.

So we live constantly between the times, and some times are obviously more pregnant with significance than others depending on the content of the past and the expectation of the future, whether that future holds judgment or promise. For the student, the days before examinations are pregnant because of imminent judgment. The days before a wedding are pregnant, too (allegorically, of course!), because of imminent promise and fulfillment.

But in the New Testament and in the early days of the church, men sensed that they were living in pregnant times all the time—in an ultimate sense. Their immediate past was ultimately significant because God had invaded the world in a child at Bethlehem; he had lived, died, and risen again. And they lived each moment in the afterglow of this utterly unbelievable invasion of time by eternity.

5

But they lived not only in the glow of a tremendous event in the past. Immediately they coupled this past event with a future event of ultimate significance too, what they called the second coming of Christ, the end of the age when the kingdom Christ had established in their hearts would be fulfilled in the last judgment on evil and in the establishment of a world of perfect love and service to others, a world of peace when there would be constant joy and singing in the streets. They were living between the ultimate times and so every "now" for them was ultimately crucial and urgent. There is, consequently, a breathless quality, a living on tiptoe, with the skin fairly prickling at the thought of what had happened and of what was still to come, which haunts the pages of the New Testament. And you and I, living in more prosy days, find it difficult to recapture or even to understand.

And this for two reasons. First, the writers of the New Testament were so overwhelmed by the display of God's power over the world and history, by this invasion of time by eternity in the coming of Christ, that they were dead sure the culmination of it all would come in their lifetime. Christ *was* coming soon for them. It was simply inconceivable that what God had started he would not finish up in a hurry! But in time they learned that they were mistaken as to the when. And after two thousand years, you and I can never recapture this same sense of urgency with respect to the when. But this is of minor importance.

The second—and vitally important—reason for their sense of urgency and living on tiptoe in expectation, was their *desire* for it to come—not for release or reward, primarily, because it included judgment. They wanted it to come because the fulfillment of what they had already experienced was so infinitely desirable. And this is something we can possibly recapture. Today we attempt to echo that urgency in the prayer, "Thy kingdom come," and in the carol, "O Come, O Come Emmanuel," which express intense desire and longing for the new age, for the kingdom of God to come in power and great glory, for all that to come that we think of when we think of heaven.

But as soon as we mention heaven, then the old cliché of the scoffers crops up: "Pie in the sky by and by." Actually, this is an empty jibe nowadays because it overlooks judgment, but even more because our customary images of heaven prove the pie to be singularly unpalatable stuff. I don't know about you, but our customary images of heaven excite no great longing or desire in me at any rate. Who wants to spend an eternity standing around clad in white robes, holding on to a palm or a harp, singing hallelujahs world without end? I know that some people for whom life has been a long, tough struggle with disappointment, frustration, and pain, may well be intrigued and comforted by a picture of eternal rest and feasting, an infinity of relaxation. But even they, I suspect, would get bored after a few thousand years of it.

The difficulty, of course, is to attempt to picture that which is beyond time and beyond our experience. The perfection of heaven presumably must be changeless because any change implies imperfection. But is the only solution to "freeze" time? To stand, sing, feast, rest—endlessly?

Keats may find delight in the frozen motion of the figures on the Grecian urn. Yet even he has to attempt to breathe some life and movement into the frozen figures:

the musician "for ever piping songs for ever new"; and the lovers "for ever panting and for ever young" even though they can never kiss. Can we do less in our imagery of heaven? For if our pictures of heaven do not excite any longing or desire, if it is all motionless, for example, then something's wrong with the picture.

Since we are time-bound and cannot think apart from time even though we know that God is above and beyond time, let us acknowledge this frankly and boldly in our pictures of heaven. For what is so unpalatable about our pictures of heaven is not that they are timeless but that they involve an interminable length of time. Therefore, let us be as bold as some of the New Testament writers who often picture heaven in terms of movement and change, even in terms of growth and development and discovery. Paul, for example, in one remarkable passage in the third chapter of Ephesians, suggests that those in the heavenly places continue to learn more about the ways and will of God as they watch his will working itself out here on earth. This suggests that there is more to learn about God—about reality!—even after we have seen him "face to face," infinite mysteries still to be unfolded, thus preserving for heaven one of the priceless joys of life on earth—the joy of discovery. Or take John's bold and gaudy picture of the New Jerusalem, a new heaven and a new earth: Here is a city with all it suggests of bustling activity, common concerns, common life. The gates of the city are open for the constant stream of newcomers. You don't have to stretch the imagination very far to picture the concern for those who have not yet arrived, and then, upon arrival, the joyful welcome, with reunions perhaps and sharing of experiences. The image of the tree of life with its leaves for "the healing of the nations" gives concrete expression to a loving concern for arrivals who are footsore, torn, weary, and heavy-laden. Worship in the heavenly city—as here—involves more than singing; it involves hearts and hands. There is much to do in heaven, thank heaven! And the much to do is precisely that which we find here most infinitely worthwhile.

Now here is a cluster of images which picture far more accurately those hints and intimations of heaven we are granted here on earth. It is the fulfillment of all those things which God has disclosed to us in the coming of Christ and which we know in our hearts to be infinitely desirable. Here then is a divine interplay of love in action and adoration, of service and song, of discovery and celebration, of concern on the part of those who have arrived for those of us still here on earth, echoing our Lord when he said, "There is joy in the presence of the angels of God over one sinner that repenteth." Imagine: All heaven bursting forth into a rush of Hallelujahs—even now—because of you, perhaps. This may be a little embarrassing, of course, especially for those of us who like to think of our religion in more anonymous terms, as of no possible interest to anyone except ourselves!

Now it was some such imagery of heaven which made the second coming of Christ not merely urgent in terms of time, but infinitely urgent in terms of desirability for the early Christians and for a whole host of Christians ever since.

Now what about you—and me? Each one of us is living between the times and even now is leaning on the future, looking for some kind of heaven. The only question that remains is what kind of a heaven do you picture for yourself in your future?

The possibility of hell, of course, is simply the fulfill-ment of a heaven of your own making. And there's no comfort in the hope expressed by the tired cliché that you'll find plenty of company in hell. Hell is always soli-tary. T. S. Eliot says somewhere that "Hell is alone." Whereas heaven is a community of love and joy which God has prepared.

However you may picture your heaven, heaven for the early Christians had tang and zest. It was no pie in the sky for them, a secure spot to which they would one day es-cape. Rather did it give ultimate significance to a present "now" which was set about by risk and danger and death. In fact, it was precisely because they had learned to think less and less about themselves and what was going to hap-pen to them, and more and more about truth and justice and love, about judgment and forgiveness, that heaven was so real to them not just in a far off future, but in the pres-ent here and now. So Paul addresses the early Christians as those "on whom the end of the age has already come" and then writes, echoing this urgency of living between the times, "Now is the accepted time." In the Greek, the word "now" sounds like the tolling of a bell: *Nun* is the accepted time; *nun* is the day of salvation. And they didn't ask for whom the bell tolled; they knew!

It tolls for you and me too, this everlasting "now." And the quality of this present "now," this time between the times, depends not only on the past but ultimately upon the picture of heaven that the future holds for you. It all depends in the end, doesn't it, upon how much urgency we can actually bring to the ancient Advent prayer: *Marana-tha!* O Lord, Come!

The God of Hope

May the God of hope fill you with all joy and peace in believing, so that by the power of the Holy Spirit you may abound in hope.   —*Romans 15:13*

"The God of hope"—that's really a strange phrase when you come to think about it for a moment. Because for a lot of us the word "God" has substance, reality, stability. "God is my rock," "my fortress," "my high tower," "God was in Christ. . . ." But "hope"—good heavens! How insubstantial and contradictory and vacillating are our hopes. I hope it won't rain tomorrow but the farmer hopes it will. The business man hopes for a good solid margin of profit while the workingman hopes for higher wages and shorter hours. A youngster hopes for a sports car while the father hopes the boy will grow up hard working and responsible. The Negro hopes for radical justice and the equality of opportunity which is his by right while the white man hopes he won't cause too much trouble. How can we possibly link God to all these myriad and conflicting hopes without splitting God up into a hopeless and meaningless schizophrenic, or else end up by tying God to each insubstantial and contradictory hope like a string trailing a balloon up into the sky? "The God of hope." It is a strange phrase, indeed.

And does it help a great deal to put the phrase into its

Advent setting where it belongs? For Advent is, of course, the season of hope. We look forward hopefully to the Coming One on Christmas: "The hopes and fears of all the years are met in thee tonight!" But we've been singing that carol for decades. And for generations before that, going back into the dark ages and beyond, ordinary people like you and me have had our hopes raised each year as Christmas approaches, hoping that it—that the Coming One—will make a difference. But has it really? Apart from a warm glow which often doesn't even outlast the fading streaks in the western sky on Christmas Day, what difference has this succession of Christmases really made?

Maybe that's why the Jews have rejected our Christ as the Coming One who when he came was actually going to bring in the kingdom of God, a time when "justice shall roll down like waters and righteousness like an everflowing stream." Where is the reign of justice? Where is the kingdom of God on earth? We've still got sin and death and injustice and suffering and the endless jockeying for power in high places and low. Is it not sheer sentimentality to pin our hopes to the Coming One at Christmas? Will things be different on December 26?

The content of the Advent hope is not exhausted, of course, in the hopes pinned to the coming of the Christ child. It always looks beyond to the event described in that cryptic phrase, the "second coming" of Christ, that moment at the end of time when God will actually establish his kingdom of righteousness and peace. On the roof of the Riverside Church in New York, just around the corner from where I live is the figure of the Angel Gabriel, his horn lifted to his mouth, ready to give out with a mighty blast to announce the second coming of our Lord in glory. Day after day he stands there at the ready. Warmed by the summer sun, frozen by winter sleet, year after year goes by, but there is no mighty blast. Not even a tentative toot. Below him are the streets of the city crawling with traffic, edged with apartment houses and slums harboring birth and death and love and conflict and a thousand shattered hopes between dawn and sunset every day. What is this hope in the second coming of Christ at the end of time—even if we can find our way through the puzzling imagery the "second coming" suggests, whether for you and me at the moment of death or for history when the curtain is rung down on the perplexing drama of human life—what is this hope but feeble, wishful thinking? A desperate effort to escape this present world where we sweat and groan and laugh at times, only to dissolve in tears at the last. Is it any more than a fainthearted whistling in the dark? A hope, to be sure, but a hope without substance, without any relevance for life here and now, little more than a "cheer up," one day it will all be over?

"The God of hope." What shall we make of it? What is Paul getting at here when he writes, "May the God of hope fill you with all joy and peace in believing, so that by the power of the Holy Spirit you may abound in hope?"

Let's begin by noting that hope is always born on a darkened stage. One biblical scholar has noted that in the Old Testament, words like "wait" and "hope" increase in number and depth in periods of the decline and fall of

Judah. Hope begins with trouble. And without denying anything that we have said about the possibility of the Christian hope being nothing more than whistling in the dark, we can also say quite frankly and without apology that hope begins when our backs are against the wall of a dead-end street and there's no other way out but to hope. I know some of the objections to this: The college student says that Christianity, when it talks about a future hope, is nothing but a crutch for weaklings who can no longer stand on their own two feet; or the skeptic says this is nothing but mumbo jumbo, swinging God in from the wings of the stage at the end of the play as a kind of celestial trouble shooter to get us out of a jam.

Well, maybe so. But may it not also be true that the Bible reads life with a deeper realism? For it recognizes our inveterate desire to keep matters in our own hands, to ignore the God who made us, to fashion the future according to our own little schemes and dreams until we end up in a mess so deep we cannot possibly struggle out of it on our own. The point is that God respects the freedom he gave us way back at the beginning. He doesn't bully us into turning to him. He isn't forever pulling and hauling to keep us out of trouble, reminding us like a petulant playwright that he's the author of the show. He treats us as free men, as truly human beings. But maybe when we have reached a point where we can see nothing but darkness and trouble, we will raise our eyes for once and discover him standing there.

So perhaps we can say that the very possibility of hope is a divine gift and that a man "must live by hope if he is to live at all." For it is precisely in the darkened corner of a dead-end street that hope provides an open door to new and unexpected possibilities. Is this just wishful thinking or is it sheerest realism?

For consider another thing, the extraordinary dynamic which hope provides. Behind the surging demands for civil rights on the part of Negroes in America, behind the young nations struggling to their feet in Africa, yes, and behind the appeal of communism in Cuba or China or Latin America is the extraordinary dynamic of hope: the hope that in the darkness of poverty and hunger and injustice there is a door which leads to a tomorrow that must be different—and better—than today. This is not wishful thinking. This is sheerest realism. Hope is indeed a divine gift. To be sure we can misuse it and distort it. We can play on the hope of desperate people to manipulate and deceive them. But this does not deny the fact of hope as a divine gift which can lift a man out of the darkness of today into the new and unexpected possibilities which tomorrow holds. Most of us simply could not live if there were no tomorrow.

But surely this is far short of what Paul means when he speaks of "the God of hope." For even if we grant that hope is a divine gift, born in the darkened corner of a dead-end street, are we not back at the point where every hope a man may have can then be called divine? What kind of "God of hope" is left? No. Paul links hope with "believing," with faith. For the Christian, the two can never be separated. We can distinguish between them only as we distinguish present from future. Hope is faith written in the future tense.

This means that hope is informed by the content of

what we believe. It has roots. It has substance. If faith is the description of our relationship to God in the here and now, an utter dependence upon and surrender to him and his will of love now; then hope is utter dependence upon and surrender to him and his will of love for the future. This is why for the Christian, hope is not simply wishful thinking, as in the TV Western, that everything will turn out all right for the "good guys" in the end—and you and I always picture ourselves as the good guys! This kind of hope is indeed an insubstantial balloon with God trailing along at the end of the string.

For mark this: If trouble breeds hope and our hopes almost invariably picture us as getting out of trouble, the content of our faith gives us no such assurance. To be sure we are given the promise of a day when God will wipe all tears from our eyes. But this promise pours us back into life around us with all its tragic evil and conflict. "For the joy that was set before him" Jesus endured the cross.

Any hopes that we may have—born and bred as they are in the darkness of suffering or illness or defeat or frustration—that we shall avoid further suffering and illness and defeat and frustration are simply not informed and shaped by our faith. God promises no one that life will be easy. But he does promise not only a way through the difficulties, but the strength and the courage to enter into the struggle with all the dark powers of life and death knowing that the darkness does not have the last word.

Thus it is futile, wishful thinking on the part of any white man—or Negro for that matter—to delude himself that the hope for racial justice will come without struggle and pain and suffering. Change can be painful. And to think we can avoid pain by stretching the process of change over an endless period of time is, in effect, to deny the possibility of change. It would be pleasant if a baby could grow into a man—with all the radical changes that go on in that process—without pain or suffering or difficulty. It would be nice. But it just isn't so. You know it and I know it.

So with your life and mine. The Christian's hope—informed, shaped, filled by the content of our faith—does not get us out of trouble. It pours us back into the struggle. It was hope—informed, shaped, filled by the content of his faith—which drove Jesus into the wilderness to be tempted, into the agony of the garden, into the forsaken loneliness of the cross. It was more than faith, commitment, and obedience to God's will of love for him in the present struggle; something was to come of all the struggle and suffering in the end—in the future. But that future hope was shaped by the content of his faith.

So even the Christian hope that looks to the end of things—to death and beyond—does not guarantee that we have an immortal soul which death cannot touch. Faith declares that God is the only one that death cannot touch. Even our Lord was not immune to death and destruction. The Christian hope says no more than that as I am utterly and completely dependent on God now for life and breath, so also at the hour of death. There is nothing in me that death cannot utterly shatter. But as I trust him now, so will I trust him then. I have no claim on him now. I have no claim on him then, no immortal soul that demands of him that death cannot touch my innermost being. But I am given the hope of resurrection from the grave if I trust him now and trust him then, which simply means that death is not the last word in the vocabulary of life.

Now the character of God's faithfulness to me is love. And so any hopes I have that are informed, shaped, filled by the content of our faith will be characterized by love. And that sharpens and defines and gives substance to these insubstantial hopes of ours even more. What are your hopes for yourself in the future? Are they shallow, superficial things, informed by a desire to escape from the tough realities of a world of injustice and bewildering evil? Such hopes haven't a ghost of a chance. For if God is love—sheer outgoing, outpouring, outgiving love—then only the hopes that mirror that same outpouring, outgiving love have any substance.

Tom Dooley hoped that a hospital might serve the less fortunate in our world. That hope has substance. Helen Keller hoped—incredibly!—that in the midst of her dark and silent world she might be useful to others. That hope has substance. If we hope for peace on earth at Christmas, that hope is utter sentimentality unless the hope has the substance of outgoing love in the form of the never-ending battle for justice, a willingness to explore all the bewildering political, economic, and diplomatic channels by which justice—food, jobs, housing, mutual respect—can be won little by little for all the peoples on the face of the earth.

Now it is this kind of hope—informed and shaped by faith and therefore filled by love—that Paul says "gives peace and joy in believing." Joy and peace obviously do not represent a shallow optimism. Rather do they indicate that all our strivings here and now to accomplish God's will of love, all of our patient endurance of suffering, the constant struggle to trust God with our lives—these are not meaningless gropings for a good that never comes. For there is no lost good. It is precisely at the end of Paul's great chapter on the resurrection (I Cor. 15), on the content of the Christian hope, that he declares: "Therefore, my beloved brethren, be ye stedfast, unmoveable, always abounding in the work of the Lord, forasmuch as ye know that your labour is not in vain in the Lord." There is no lost good. And is this not one of the primary implications of the second coming of Christ, if we can penetrate its puzzling and baffling imagery? Whatever else it may mean, it means that God is in control of the future as well as of the present. His will of love will not be thwarted endlessly. And every reflection of that love that he has for us which gleams through our struggles in the dark here and now is a foretaste—an actualized anticipation of his ultimate victory.

For you can actually *taste* the future fulfillment in the present moment. To be sure, there is the taste of death in the mouth too. But there is also the taste of life, a foretaste of the future fulfillment—of victory, of the kingdom come—present here and now.

Perhaps you may have tasted it as I have at the communion table, where through eating and drinking we participate not only in the death, "proclaiming his death," but also the resurrection, "till he come."

But foretaste is not fulfillment. An eschatology—theological jargon for the last things, death and what may come afterward—an eschatology which finds the future *only* in the present lacks the zest and anticipation of a "foretaste," of more to come, and fails to reflect the eagerness with which the early church awaited that future to come when indeed there would be "no more sea" and "all tears would be wiped from their eyes." So they prayed, not to escape the present now, nor to see all possibility limited to the present now, but because what they tasted now of God's ultimate victory filled them with a zest for so much more. They prayed, *Maranatha*—O Lord quickly come!

I wonder sometimes whether the current disillusionment with the church is due not merely to all the obvious reasons we know by heart, but also to a truncated version of the Christian faith which though so obviously in desperate earnest about the present now, full of divine possibilities, is unable to see anything beyond the now. It's a kind of faith without hope which engenders a feverish concentration on the moment, and because the present moment yields only a foretaste may end in frustration. This feverish concentration on the present is not unlike a condemned man eating his last meal. We are not condemned men, obviously, but sometimes we look as if we were, in our fixation upon the present to the neglect of the future.

The Christian sees the present not merely as a last meal to be savored to the full, but also as a foretaste of an unimaginable banquet feast which will not have to be eaten in the shadow of death. May it not be true that the Christian hope actually takes a more realistic view of life here and now, takes the inevitable tension of the life of faith more seriously, than those who would try feverishly to abolish the tension in capturing life abundant in the fullness of all its dimensions here and now? Does not hope, without undercutting the crucial importance of the present moment for faith, yet release us from the other peril of refusing to let God be God of the future as well as of the present? God always has more in store for us—even, perhaps, within the structure of the suburban church!

Or to change the figure, we are not destined to remain forever gripped by the birth pangs of the new creation coming into being in life and in society here and now; one day the birth pangs will be over. Meanwhile the pain is pregnant with anticipation for joy that a man—a new creation in all the fullness of the stature of Christ—will be born.

Perhaps the figure of the Angel Gabriel standing high above the streets of New York, his horn raised to his lips, is not so ridiculous or irrelevant after all. For that figure, high above the city below, is the constant reminder, day in and day out, year in and year out, through summer sun and winter sleet, that God's will of love *will* be done. And although the dust and dirt of life in the streets below, the shattered dreams, the sleazy lives, the smell of death, may seem to mock it and deny it, here is the assurance that Christ was not born in vain and those who give themselves to his life of love do not live in vain or die in vain. Christmas is always the foretaste of more to come.

So there is a deep and underlying joy and peace to the life of faith here and now. We need not despair nor need we get all hot and breathless as if the issue of it all were in our hands alone. It's not. The fulfillment of life and history is in his hands. And you and I ought to be content to leave it there. Someone once asked Luther, "Tell me what would you do today if you were absolutely convinced that tomorrow would bring the end of the world?" Luther replied, "I would plant a tree." "Joy and peace in believing!"

So we live, "abounding in hope," a hope that is given substance by what God has done for us in Christ, by what he is doing now for us in Christ, and by what he still holds in store for those who trust themselves to his faithful and unchanging love. And now "may the God of hope fill you with all joy and peace in believing"—in your struggle to be faithful to him here and now.

Voices in the Dark

Comfort, comfort my people,
  says your God.
Speak tenderly to Jerusalem,
  and cry to her
that her warfare is ended,
  that her iniquity is pardoned,
that she has received from the Lord's hand
  double for all her sins.

A voice cries:
"In the wilderness prepare the way of the Lord,
  make straight in the desert a highway for our God.
Every valley shall be lifted up,
  and every mountain and hill be made low;
the uneven ground shall become level,
  and the rough places a plain.
And the glory of the Lord shall be revealed,
  and all flesh shall see it together,
  for the mouth of the Lord has spoken."

A voice says, "Cry!"
  And I said, "What shall I cry?"
All flesh is grass,
  and all its beauty is like the flower of the field.
The grass withers, the flower fades,
  when the breath of the Lord blows upon it;
  surely the people is grass.
The grass withers, the flower fades;
  but the word of our God will stand for ever.
                                    —*Isaiah 40:1-8*

I wonder whether you are aware of the important role that darkness plays in the story of Christmas. A dark stable in the dead of night is the traditional setting. The darkened sky overarching the shepherds is shattered by the glory of angels. A midnight sky sets off the star which leads the wise men to the place. Christmas is essentially a night festival. People have an instinct for this: they crowd the churches in the midnight darkness where candles gleam in a shadowy church. But they stay away in droves from services on Christmas Day held in broad daylight.

To be sure a lot of this is sheer sentiment. Candles look pretty. Christmas Day services interfere with family celebrations. And it is a bit exotic to troop off to church in the middle of the night. But this is more than just tradition or sentiment. There is a sense in which the symbolism of darkness is essential if we are to understand what Christmas is all about. I have sometimes wondered how much more difficult it must be to catch the meaning of Christmas in lands where daylight lingers far into the night at this time of year.

As a matter of fact, one of our difficulties right here and now in preparing for Christmas is that there are far too many lights around: in store windows, in garlands thrown across the streets, on trees in city squares, in windows and on roofs. It's all a little too gay and festive—too soon!

We have already seen that hope is born in the darkened corner of a dead-end street. This is authentic. At Christmas the hope is given a voice. And the voice is heard more distinctly and clearly in the silent darkness. Indeed, this is the way the voice of God is always heard most distinctly and clearly—in the dark.

Now I want to take you back hundreds of years before the birth of Christ to a prophet who heard voices in the dark. It may help us to prepare for Christmas in a way no amount of bustling about, hanging out lights, shopping for presents, mailing out cards, and all the rest of it can ever do.

For fifty years the chosen people of God had been living in exile in Babylon. Fifty years—that's a long time in any man's life. Almost two generations. Most of the people then alive had never known the glories of Jerusalem, the gleaming city God had given them with its temple, the place where behind drawn curtains God was truly present. Death had been busy during those fifty years, and now only the older generation could tell unbelieving youngsters about the glory of the past and the nearness of God which had once been theirs. No wonder the youngsters were incredulous. There had been no voice from God in this strange and godless land for half a century. Not even a whisper. So they sat in the darkness by the rivers of Babylon and wept, longing for a voice—even a whisper—that God was still alive; that he still cared; that he was still faithful to the covenant he had made with their ancient forefathers, Abraham, Isaac, and Jacob. Or had it all been delusion, superstition, legend?

It is in this darkness of a people forgotten, bewildered, disillusioned, that a prophet heard a voice, soft and clear: "Comfort ye, comfort ye my people, speak ye tenderly. . . ." Tell them that their exile is ended, their iniquity pardoned. The voice broke in on the darkness of their despair as softly and gently as a child born in the outbuildings of a village inn. Away from the noisy jokes and laughter of transients gathered about the tavern bar, "How silently, how silently, the wondrous gift is given." It's not that God isn't concerned about the noisy transients at the bar; it's just that his voice—the first voice we ever hear from him—comes more clearly in the silent darkness of life.

But is this really so? Where in these busy, frantic weeks before Christmas are we most apt to hear the authentic voice of God? In the breathless rush of shopping? In the crowded and frenetic stores? In the noisy parties and joyful reunions of separated families? Quite possibly so. But the authentic voice of God is heard most clearly in the dark. Look around you for a moment. Soak yourself in the darkness of life, if you've the stomach for it: the unemployed man huddled on a park bench staring vacantly into nothingness; the hospital for incurables with the patients ticking off the endless minutes until the end; the city slums hopelessly caught in the web of racial, political, and social structures that apparently offer no hope. Or, if you'd rather, simply listen to the daily newscast—almost any day will do: fire breaks out, twenty families homeless; civil rights bill caught in hopeless tangle in Washington; Dow Jones industrial average drops 5½ points; committee investigates construction graft in city schools; seven die in local highway accidents over weekend. Then, in the darkness of these days, listen to a voice: "Comfort ye, comfort ye my people, speak ye tenderly . . . saith your God." Is this really the voice of God? Does he really care?

The only assurance we have is that this is the way God's voice spoke in the child Jesus. No lights in the door to welcome him. Shut out into the darkness. Hounded by

Herod. Finally, spat upon, betrayed, denied, crucified. Well, what is it? The voice of God? Or a fairy story for children?

"Comfort ye, comfort ye my people." For the ancient prophet by the waters of Babylon, the voice was authentic. God had not forgotten. He is not far off in some distant temple now reduced to rubble. He is here, faithful in his love no matter how dark the days, how perplexing and baffling life may be.

Notice, too, that although the prophet hears more than one voice in the dark, the first voice he hears is the voice of comfort, of assurance. He heard other voices too there in the darkness, a voice of demand, "Prepare in the desert a highway. . . ." But the first voice was the assurance of God's faithful love. This is how God always speaks to us, in assurance and comfort first.

Strange how we churchmen have distorted this and turned it upside down. Nine out of ten people, whether inside or outside the church, will tell you that the church demands something of you, that the church is made up of people who live according to certain demands, commandments. Religion is a chore and a burden. You have to give up some rather enticing vices. God comes with a demand in his fist. In a moving documentary describing the East Harlem Protestant Parish in the slums of New York, one of the most revealing scenes pictured the reluctance of a woman to let a minister inside the door of her shabby apartment. She knew he must be wanting something from her. It took a year for her to be broken down to the realization that this church at least, unlike every other part of the world she knew, was demanding nothing. It simply wanted to offer what she didn't have, love, friendship, the security of a community which cared about her and her children.

How we have mangled the New Testament. For at every step of the way—and not only in the New Testament—it is the voice of "Comfort ye, comfort ye my people" which comes first. God delivered the people from slavery in Egypt before the ten commandments were given. The gift of the child at Bethlehem came before the call to take up his cross. The invitation to the wedding feast came before the demand for a wedding garment.

But even in your own life you may know this to be true. Perhaps you are one of the lucky ones who were loved and cared for before the demand for obedience came from your parents. And it was only the prior care and love that gave validity to the demand. God makes his demands, to be sure, and we'll come to that in a moment. But first—always first—is the assurance of his faithful love. And we can receive that assurance, hear the voice of comfort most clearly when we are in the dark, when nothing we do seems to make much sense, when anything demanded of us brings nothing but frustration.

So as we prepare for his coming at Christmas he doesn't demand that we clean ourselves up, like a church preparing for the visit of a bishop, or a housewife taking her hair out of curlers for a visit from the minister. He asks only that we be prepared to receive, to be open to the possibility of his love.

Then what about the second voice? "In the wilderness prepare the way of the Lord." Isn't this a demand? Is the assurance of love simply another example of the soft sell? A softening up before we are hit with the demand? No. The point is that we are not capable of receiving the love without the demand. A psychiatrist tells of a youngster with a serious emotional disturbance who described his problem: "My parents never tell me what to do or what not to do. They always let me do whatever I like. I wish I were free like other boys." Love that makes no demands is not love. It is wishy-washy sentimentality and destroys rather than recreates.

Re-creation occurs only when we recognize that the voice of demand, "In the wilderness prepare . . . ," is the other side of the voice of assurance, "Comfort ye my people." For how can we possibly appropriate the assurance, how can we possibly know it is really so, unless we give ourselves to it in response? I suppose most of us have attempted at one time or another to console a bereaved father, mother, wife, husband, and had the experience of the futility of it all when nothing happened. Our words seemed to bounce off and leave a hollow echo in the room. And so they did until the one in darkness made the venture of response in picking up the pieces of his life and began to act as if the voice of comfort were more than empty sounds, were an actual clue to the meaning of his life.

So with God. How can we know that the God who assures us of his love in a manger is really a God of love unless we give ourselves to the love? So it was with the exiles in the darkness of Babylon. The only way they could receive the voice of assurance was to act on the voice of demand, "In the wilderness prepare. . . ."

To be sure, it was a crazy kind of demand. Here they

were, lonely, cut off from home, longing for the good old days, surrounded by pagans who didn't care a rap about them or their God, and yet with it all they had managed a modicum of security and comfort. Then came the voice of comfort and with it the voice of demand that they pull up their families, forego what little comfort and security they had, and start back across the trackless desert—to what? To a Jerusalem sacked and plundered and to a temple in ruins. What sense did it make? No wonder most of them said, "No thanks. We'll sit it out here in Babylon."

But isn't this always the way the assurance of God's love makes its crazy demand? In the wilderness of life around us which seems to lead nowhere? In the hopeless wilderness of relations between East and West? In the tangled, trackless wilderness of race relations? In the baffling wilderness of the business world where a man simply has to beat his competitor to the draw if he is to survive? In the overwhelming wilderness of the population explosion? In the bleak wilderness of a marriage headed for the rocks?

It's not surprising that a lot of us too would rather sit tight in whatever little comfort and security we have been able to carve out of the jungle of life, shut our eyes and ears to the confusing and frightening wilderness around us, and cultivate a cozier religion which is content to show up in church, tithe perhaps, send the kids to Sunday school, and cultivate a wistful picture of a God who somehow, if we play it safe, will see to it that the wilderness will take care of itself and we'll come through it all relatively untouched and unharmed.

But as someone has said, "On the back of a voice which sets our heart right with God ('Comfort ye my people') comes a voice to set the world right ('In the wilderness prepare . . .') and no man is godly who has not heard both.'" And what is more, no one can really know the comfort and assurance of God's love until he has answered the demand in the wilderness of life around him to prepare. For is God's love sovereign over all of life or isn't it? Is there a loving purpose to be found in all the bewildering problems of life around us in the twentieth century, or isn't there? What is the use of a divine love that gives me assurance and hope in the midst of my own personal problems and perplexities but which has nothing to do with feeding an exploding population, nothing to do with families crowded into slums, nothing to do with the dignity of a man whose skin is darker than others? If God's love is not sovereign there in the wilderness, it's not the love of God, Lord of nature and all history. And he's certainly not the God of the Bible who comes down into the wilderness of life's perplexities and savage tragedy as a child in a stable.

Does this mean, then, that we Christians are supposed to have all the answers to life's big and knotty problems? No. Listen to the prophet for there is a strange twist in the demand to prepare:

> "In the wilderness prepare the way of the Lord;
>   make straight in the desert a highway for our God.
> Every valley shall be lifted up
>   and every mountain and hill be made low;
> the uneven ground shall become level,
>   and the rough places a plain."

[1] George Adam Smith, *The Book of Isaiah* (New York: Harper, n.d.), II, 81.

Do you see the twist? Following the demand to prepare, the demand to give ourselves to the claims of love
and justice in the wilderness, is the assurance that God is
in it, solving the problems, removing the obstacles. *We*
don't lift the valleys and remove the mountains, level off
the rough places; he does. We're not called to build the
kingdom of God on earth; that's his domain. We can't
reconcile estranged people or estranged groups in our
country. That's his business.

I think it is precisely at this point that we may have
misunderstood the mission of the church in the world.
Some of us have said that when it comes to the race problem, or political problems like slums and schools, our mission is to change the hearts of men and not get involved
with sit-in demonstrations or political machines. But what
kind of presumption is this, that it's our task to reconcile
man to man? The prophet says, rather, that the demand
upon us is to prepare—to act—and precisely in the wilderness of life. The rest is in God's hands.

This means that if we are to prepare, we are to respond
to God's assurance of his love in loving involvement in
the wilderness of life around us, whether it be in political
activity or in demonstrations against injustice of whatever
kind, or in the hard ethical decisions of business, or in
whatever need the community in which we live places before us. Opportunities vary with each community and each
individual. It certainly means that we do not prepare by
sitting tight in our secure little churches, fearful of the
wilderness around us.

Does this seem a strange way to prepare for the coming
of the Christ child on Christmas? Maybe so. But it seemed

mighty strange to the exiles in Babylon, too. But those who ventured on the basis of God's "Comfort ye" to "Prepare in the wilderness" found the comfort to be authentic. God did care and he still does. No matter how dark the night or how bleak the wilderness, the voice comes soft and clear in a child in a manger: "I am come that ye might have life. . . . Take up your cross and follow me."

The Mystery of Christ

For this reason I, Paul, a prisoner for Christ Jesus on behalf of you Gentiles—assuming that you have heard of the stewardship of God's grace that was given to me for you, how the mystery was made known to me by revelation, as I have written briefly. When you read this you can perceive my insight into the mystery of Christ, which was not made known to the sons of men in other generations as it has now been revealed to his holy apostles and prophets by the Spirit; that is, how the Gentiles are fellow heirs, members of the same body, and partakers of the promise in Christ Jesus through the gospel.

Of this gospel I was made a minister according to the gift of God's grace which was given me by the working of his power. To me, though I am the very least of all the saints, this grace was given, to preach to the Gentiles the unsearchable riches of Christ, and to make all men see what is the plan of the mystery hidden for ages in God who created all things; that through the church the manifold wisdom of God might now be made known to the principalities and powers in the heavenly places. This was according to the eternal purpose which he has realized in Christ Jesus our Lord, in whom we have boldness and confidence of access through our faith in him. So I ask you not to lose heart over what I am suffering for you, which is your glory.

For this reason I bow my knees before the Father, from whom every family in heaven and on earth is named, that according to the riches of his glory he may grant you to be strengthened with might through his Spirit in the inner man, and that Christ may dwell in your hearts through faith; that you, being rooted and grounded in love, may have power to comprehend with all the saints what is the breadth and length and height and depth, and to know the love of Christ which surpasses knowledge, that you may be filled with all the fullness of God.

Now to him who by the power at work within us is able to do far more abundantly than all that we ask or think, to him be glory in the church and in Christ Jesus to all generations, for ever and ever. Amen.   —*Ephesians 3:1-21*

It's no secret that this is an age of slide rules and computers, of sharp sociological surveys and analyses based on meticulous case studies, an age of weights and measures and facts. We depend upon Consumer's Research before buying and on critical reviews before venturing to the book stall, theatre, or even to the TV set. We look at the world through narrowed eyelids. We're not about to be taken in by God, the Bible, the church, or the corner supermarket —not if we can help it!

And all of this is more than necessary, especially in the church and among Christians who have too often been led off by the nose into blind alleys and irrelevancies by woolly thinking, purple pulpit rhetoric, vague generalities, and unexamined claims and assumptions.

But it is precisely in such an age that we also need to be reminded ever and again of the surrounding mystery. And so just now I propose that we do no more than celebrate— not delineate or analyze or examine but celebrate the surrounding mystery in life, in God, in Christ, in the church, as this celebration of the surrounding mystery comes to the surface in the third chapter of Ephesians.

Someone has said that sometimes Paul's words "come

as water jets in uneven spurts from a bottle held upside down."[1] Such is unquestionably the case here in this third chapter of Ephesians, a passage which is the utter despair of the expositor. For what preacher has not vainly tried to catch something of the soaring incandescence of just one of these phrases: "According to the riches of his glory he may grant you to be strengthened with might through his Spirit in the inner man," or "rooted and grounded in love, may have power to comprehend with all the saints what is the breadth and length and height and depth," or "able to do far more abundantly than all that we ask or think." To draw out some of the breathless implications in just one of those soaring phrases is one thing; to attempt to expose the implications in all of them as they are set in the context of the "mystery hidden for ages in God who created all things" is quite an impossible other.

And yet it seems to me that moving through this magnificent chapter there is a celebration of the surrounding mystery as discernible progression, not to be found in a pedantic, chronological, verse-by-verse procession, but still discernibly there. The progression begins with the dark mystery of a plan "hidden for ages in God," then moves through a mysteriously bright disclosure in the "unsearchable riches of Christ," and culminates in the continuing mystery here and now of a God "able to do far more abundantly than all that we ask or think according to the power that worketh in us." Although the passage is enfolded in mystery, its thought is not hopelessly mysterious.

We begin, then, with the "plan of the mystery hidden

[1] Quoted by Joseph Sittler in *The Ecology of Faith* (Philadelphia: Muhlenberg, 1961), p. 54.

for ages in God who created all things." Here is the murky darkness of all the unanswered questions in which human life is caught: What is life all about? Why are we here? What is the purpose lying behind birth and life, behind joy and laughter, suffering and death? Prodded and probed by these haunting questions, the human story has left its monuments to the search for answers: Shakespeare and Goethe and Karl Marx, the Taj Mahal and Buddhist temples, Plato and Confucius, Hitler, Sartre, the welfare state, and the rise of nationalism in Africa today. All of them in some sense have been trying to find the answer to the "plan of the mystery hidden for ages in God who created all things."

For some, of course, the seeking has resulted only in unrelieved darkness. There is no answer. Life is a mockery, and absurdity. And if there is a God "who created all things," which is doubtful, he must be a monster, laughing hideously at our puny efforts to control cancer and heart disease or the hydrogen bomb. The mystery lies enshrouded in unrelieved darkness. And what honest man will not acknowledge the appeal of this grim answer in certain moments, at least, when the whole business makes absolutely no sense at all.

For others, the mystery is a shadowy never-never land. In Gibbon's *Decline and Fall,* it is set down: "The various modes of worship which prevailed in the Roman world were all considered by the people as equally true, by the philosophers as equally false, and by the magistrates as equally useful."[2] A whole host of people today react in

[2] Quoted by David H. C. Read in *I Am Persuaded* (New York: Scribner, 1961), p. 56.

precisely the same way. All religions are equally true. The ways of life and God are mysterious and who can say with any authority that one religion is superior to another, one faith more true than any other faith? Students in universities across the world press the question, and the rest of the world acts as if the question did not need to be raised: "We're all going to the same place, aren't we? Does it make any difference which road we travel?" The Christian's heaven or the Buddhist's Nirvana is the end of the road in either case. What difference does it really make? As for life here and now, who is to say? For the rank and file, all religions are equally true because they are equally mysterious. Some would say, equally superstitious. As for the philosophers, most of them still find all religions equally false. And as for the magistrates, the Union of Soviet Socialist Republics no doubt will try to find the church as useful in the long run as did the Czars, precisely as useful as the Western nations have found Protestantism to be on occasion for the shoring up of democracy. Life may be mysterious and no one may be able to say precisely what lies behind the shadowy mystery, but religion is useful, at least, both to the common man and to the magistrate, and let the philosophers play with their skeptical blocks.

But into this shadowy never-never land, into the unrelieved darkness, the light shines. For Paul it was a light in the darkness of the Damascus Road, "the mystery was made known to me by revelation." This is Christianity's incredible claim and, for a sensitive person, a continuing embarrassment, that he feels constrained to say that his faith is not one religion alongside of other religions, not *a* religion at all by which men grope through the shadows looking for life and light, but rather a gospel, a breaking in from the eternal mystery beyond. The darkness is shattered by light: "The people that walked in darkness have seen a great light." The never-never land where all religions are equally true, equally false, and equally useful is shattered by a resounding "I AM": "I AM the Lord thy God . . . I AM the way, the truth, and the life."

Now if this be so, then what is the purpose of the disclosure, this invasion of the world from beyond? For Paul the content of the mysterious plan "hidden for ages in God" and now disclosed is quite clear, even though expressed in language that seems archaic and obscure: "How the Gentiles are fellow heirs, members of the same body and partakers of the promise in Christ Jesus through the gospel." It is the all-inclusiveness of the broken walls of hostility, "neither slave nor free, Jew nor Greek." And the secret of the broken walls is the mysterious miracle of God battering down the walls of hostility inside each one of us to make us one with him and consequently one with each other, call it justification, atonement, or reconciling sacrifice. For Paul, this glad disclosure is no less than an incredibly joyous miracle. He touches it with awe and with the sense that this is holy ground. Note the awe-filled reticence in the phrases, "the mystery of Christ," the "unsearchable riches of Christ." It's as if he were afraid we might lay rude hands upon it and make of it a commonplace instead of the unspeakable God bending down to enfold us all in the arms of his love.

Speaking for my own tradition, how often we Lutherans—so unlike Luther—have torn away the mystery and made of the miracle of "justification by grace through faith" little more than a denominational identification tag, trampled on the wonder of it in dogmatic text books, flaunted it in the faces of Christian brothers as a polemical weapon, gagged and starved the life—and the mystery of God—out of it!

But are other traditions and denominations clean handed here? "Saved by grace through faith" in whatever tradition has often fallen into a lifeless formula, a proposition to be accepted by the orthodox, the test of a "gospel sermon," as if the words were of themselves an open sesame to vibrant life here and beyond.

But at this time, in this place, let us catch through Paul's soaring phrases something of the wonder and mystery of God's plan, "hidden for ages," to enfold all men in his love, even you and me. For the disclosure of the mystery of God's plan in a cross and resurrection does not dispel the mystery! The riches of God's love disclosed to us in Christ are still "unsearchable." No man can fathom them. No one—thank God—has ever really felt that he has been completely successful in explaining the inner workings of God in the mysterious action of a cross and resurrection. For God does not disclose himself in the unsearchable riches of Christ to "explain himself." He comes only to accomplish his plan, to unite us in forgiving love with himself so that we may be united in forgiving love with all the brothers of men.

But mystery is piled on mystery! Not only is the "plan of the mystery hidden in God" disclosed in the "unsearchable riches of Christ," but listen: "That the manifold wisdom of God might now be made known to the principalities and powers in the heavenly places *through the church!"* Do you see how utterly and ridiculously incongruous this is? That God—the mysterious other—by whose word this whole mysterious universe came into being, whose hand upholds the laws of nature which scientists so painfully and breathlessly trace with their computers and electronic gadgets, whose eye glances back to the day of Abraham as if it were yesterday and sees the consummation of it all at the end of time as if it were tomorrow morning—that this God should choose to make known his hidden, secret purpose, the clue to the inner meaning of life—your life, my life—through the church! Through the likes of you and me and thousands of others like us! And doing so while the world goes its busy way making money and love and revolutions and poems and skyscrapers and music and H-bombs, as if what went on in Christian communities and parish churches scattered across cities and countryside throughout the world were the least of life's side shows. But Paul says it's the main event! Even the principalities and powers in the heavenly places peek over the battlements of heaven to look down, even now—at this moment, not as in Hebrews to see how we're making out, but rather to learn more of the mysterious plan of God for the eternal destiny of the world, a mysterious secret even in the heavenlies until it works itself out through the church on earth, through you and me.

I wonder if we still have the grace to put our hands to our mouths in astonishment now and then as we contemplate the wonder of it all? That on the lips and through the lives of such ordinary people as you and me, and in the taste of bread and wine, the church makes known to the principalities and powers in the heavenly places the secret plan of God, "How the Gentiles are fellow heirs . . . partakers of the promise," that all men are to be enfolded in the love that passeth knowledge.

The curse in all this, of course, is its familiarity. The wonder that the mystery has been disclosed evaporates. The "unsearchable riches of Christ" have been dissected and analyzed in Sunday-school lessons, sermons, and Bible classes and, what is worse, made to sound dull! The incalculable mystery that the God of all power and might should choose to work his inscrutable purpose through the church has been domesticated into stewardship programs, evangelism efforts, and strategies for renewal, along with an inveterate appetite for measuring results to see whether any or all of it really works! It's all too ordinary, too familiar to evoke wonder and surprise. This is the peril of disclosure, the risk God took in revealing himself in earthen vessels, that we should take it all for granted and no longer be astonished or surprised.

Helmut Thielicke has written that "we . . . have gradually become accustomed to the dangerous and unhealthy idea that the Grace of God is thrown at us. . . . But this is not so. . . . The Grace of God can also be silent. . . . Even the most orthodox churchman will not enter the kingdom of heaven unless he is continually surprised that mercy has been shown him. . . . Perhaps God has first to be jerked away from us complacent Western Christians, like a rug from under our feet, if we are to be reawakened to this surprise."[3]

For without this surprise, this amazement at the mys-

---

[3] Helmut Thielicke, *The Silence of God* (Grand Rapids: Eerdmans, 1962), pp. 18-19. Used by permission.

terious wonder of God's strange dealings with us, we cannot appreciate the continuing mystery in our response. For only as we see the utter incongruity of the way God intends to work out his secret purpose—through the church—through us!—can we ever be open to the workings of his Spirit. So Paul prays in wonder, "I bow my knees before the Father . . . that he may grant you to be strengthened with might through his Spirit in the inner man . . . that Christ may dwell in your hearts through faith; that . . . rooted and grounded in love . . . you may be filled with all the fullness of God."

For apart from this continuing mystery of God's love constantly filling us, what possible hope is there for the church in our time? It's no trick at all to move around the churches from one country to another and see nothing but insurmountable problems: the threat of communism and nihilism without, the deadly softness of apathy within, the strident voices of ecumenical isolationism, the lack of an abundance of first-rate manpower and personnel, the narrow parochialism of clergy and people, to say nothing of the perennial lack of adequate financial resources. Taking us on a purely human level, what possible chance does God have with the likes of you and me? And the current passion for analyzing the church in suburbia, small town, rural areas, and inner city only serves to underline the desperate situation.

But with the ongoing mystery of his grace, with one life here and another there opened to all the fullness—the very "pleroma"—of God, nothing is impossible. I never fail to be astonished at what God intends to accomplish and has already accomplished through the most ordinary people. To be sure there have been great names in the history of the church: Paul, Augustine, Luther, Kierkegaard, Bonhoeffer—to restrict ourselves only to one tradition. But the mysterious ferment of God's grace working in the lives of men down through the ages would have died out long ago if he had been dependent only upon the great ones. God is pleased to work with nobodies (made abundantly clear on a winter's night when there was no room in an inn), nobodies who become somebodies when their eyes are filled with wonder at the unsearchable riches of his love and their hearts are opened to the fullness of that love so that it can no longer be contained but must spill over to break down the walls of hostility in families, communities, nations, and churches.

All he asks here is that we never lose sight of the ongoing mystery of his power working within us; never let it all go flat and stale and familiar. For the mystery of a child's cry in a stable, the mystery of an empty tomb, the mystery of tongues as of fire and a sound as of a rushing mighty wind—the mystery of that same God is present here and now, seeking, always seeking entrance. And once having entered into us, he is "able to do far more abundantly than all that we ask or think. . . ." Wherefore, my brethren, "to him be glory in the church and in Christ Jesus to all generations, for ever and ever. Amen."

Even the Winds and the Sea

And when he was entered into a ship, his disciples followed him. And, behold, there arose a great tempest in the sea, insomuch that the ship was covered with the waves: but he was asleep. And his disciples came to him, and awoke him, saying, Lord, save us: we perish. And he saith unto them, Why are ye fearful, O ye of little faith? Then he arose, and rebuked the winds and the sea; and there was a great calm. But the men marvelled, saying, What manner of man is this, that even the winds and the sea obey him!
—*Matthew 8:23-27* (KJV)

The other day I was watching a sunset out of my study window, high in a tower overlooking the Hudson River and New Jersey beyond. And the question suddenly occurred to me: What does Christ have to do with a sunset? It may seem like an odd question because we are accustomed to think of Christ in terms of Bible and church and Sunday school and prayer or in terms of our relationship to other people, to family and friends, to Negroes and Africans and Jews, and beyond that to the problems of war and peace and international relations. In all these areas of personal relationships, to think of Christ does not seem at all strange.

But what does Christ have to do with the world of nature around us which science is busily exploring with such fantastic results? What does Christ have to do with sunsets

46

or with galaxy upon galaxy of stars extending into space so vast it numbs the mind even to think of it? What does he have to do with space probes and nuclear fission and biochemistry, or with the exploration of the bottom of the sea? Sometimes, I suppose, we may think of this exciting age of scientific exploration in terms of God, but hardly ever, I suspect, in terms of Christ. Christ for the average American Christian is a far cozier word than God. Christ suggests the closeness and intimacy of a neighborhood church and its pastor, the closeness and intimacy of one who like ourselves was lonely and tempted and at the mercy of wind and rain and evil men, and consequently one to whom we turn for sympathy and understanding and love. Indeed he may be the one to whom we turn when we are frightened by the possibilities of what science is discovering these days: fifty megaton bombs, atomic fallout, guided missiles, the creation of life in a test tube, flights into space, the possible discovery of life on other planets, the establishment of space platforms circling the earth from which presumably one nation might be able to control the entire world and bring it into subjection. I suspect we are tempted to think of Christ as the victim—like ourselves—of all of these frightening developments triggered by scientific imagination and research, the victim rather than the one who made it all possible!

What, then, does Christ have to do with a sunset? Or with the galaxies of stars? Or with nuclear fission? If he has nothing to do with it, then it is easy to see why our world is plagued with the demons of greed and superstition and anxiety. The greed is all too obvious. The very mention of an oil well, for example, means but one thing

to an American—a dollar sign. And so with the rest of
our natural resources, they mean dollars primarily, and
I'm not excluding the natural resource of the loveliness of
our countryside marred and scarred by signs and billboards
and even uglier automobile graveyards. And why not, you
see, if Christ is divorced from the natural world in which
we live? If there is nothing but an "intelligence" behind
the created world around us, why should not we too apply
our intelligence, our wits and brains, to use it as we please?
And generally we "please" to turn it all into dollars as
fast as we can. Why is it that the conservation of our natural resources, whether forests or fish, wildlife or oil, always has such an uphill battle, if it is not that we have
divorced Christ from nature?

But greed is not the only result of this divorce; superstition thrives on it too. Does it not seem a little strange
to you that in this enlightened twentieth century when presumably we have grown far beyond a belief in demons,
witches, and goblins, almost every newspaper in the land
carries the daily horoscope and a column on astrology?
And yet if there is no other clue to the mystery of life except a vague and inscrutable deity called "God," then maybe I'd be tempted too to look to the mysterious heavens
for daily guidance. After all, why take any chances? And
that goes for black cats, ladders, knocking on wood, and
the number 13, too.

At a deeper level this same kind of superstitious fatalism invades the churches as well as the newspapers whenever Christ is divorced from the world around us. When
cancer strikes, or a heart attack, or there's a crack-up on
the highway, how often you hear devout people say, "Why

48

did God . . . ?" But you never hear them say, "Why did Christ . . . ?" No wonder we are ridden with fears and anxieties if we worship Christ, the loving shepherd, in church and prayer and yet so rarely connect him with the mysteries of life outside the church. If we can say of death coming suddenly and unexpectedly, "It must have been God's will . . ." and yet never bring ourselves to say, "It must have been Christ's will . . ."—then we are actually worshiping one God in church whom we call Christ, while acknowledging that in the world outside there is another unknown God who is really in charge, but whose ways and will are inscrutable and almost invariably unfriendly. So one poet pictures himself looking up into the heavens for a clue:

> Ah, in the midnight, in the dawn
> I listened—and have never heard,
> However faint or far-withdrawn,
> The vibrance of Thy summoning word!
>
> More harsh than jangled bolts and bars—
> More cruel than promises forgone—
> The senile silence of Thy stars,
> The idiot radiance of Thy dawn.[1]

Now it's against this background of a chaotic, inscrutable, and anxiety-ridden world where Christ is so readily divorced from the world of nature, that I want you to look at this striking story of Christ calming the storm on Galilee. It's one of the most familiar stories in the New Tes-

[1] Arthur Davison Ficke, "Father," from *The Secret and Other Poems* (New York: Doubleday, 1929). These, the last two stanzas, are used by permission.

tament and appears in three of the four Gospels, reasonably strong evidence that this story was deeply treasured by the early church. The usual interpretation, of course, is that there is no storm in life that can threaten us or the church because Christ is by our side to save and protect us. But the story says far more than that: It says something dramatic and startling about Christ's relationship to the natural world around him. The final exclamation of the disciples sums it up: "What manner of man is this, that even the winds and the sea obey him!" It means that our Lord is not simply one of us, bewildered victim of wind and sea and the forces of nature, but that he is more, that he is in some mysterious way linked with the very forces of nature themselves. So the author of the fourth Gospel, reflecting on this mystery declared, "He was in the beginning with God; all things were made through him and without him was not anything made that was made."

You see what this means: that the God of creation, the God of the natural world around us, is not one thing, an impersonal force or power that is as inscrutable and cold and heartless as fate, while Christ who is warm, personal, the very embodiment of love, is another. They are one and the same. It means that the God of sunset and hurricane and snowflake and the immensities of space is the same God who comes to earth in a peasant child in a Bethlehem stable. This is why this story of the stilling of the storm on Galilee has for centuries been read in most churches during the Epiphany season. It is precisely to show that we have not done with the meaning of the coming of Christ on Christmas until we have seen the relationship of the Christ in the manger to the world of nature around us, for here is another of those startling biblical paradoxes: the helpless child in a manger and the stilling of a storm on the sea. It is precisely so that we shall never forget that the child in Bethlehem who discloses the very heart of God as a love that comes down to seek out the lonely and disheartened and lost children of men—that love is the same love which is at the center of the creative power which brought the world into being at the beginning of time and sustains it in his hands until the end of time. "What manner of man is this, that even the winds and the sea obey him!"

This does not mean, of course, that the mystery of life is now swept away and all is as plain as the nose on your face. It's not, obviously. A man cannot contemplate the world of nature—a sunset or a snowflake—and come up with a God of love who created it all. A brilliant red sunset can be nothing more than the harbinger of a storm sweeping up the coast bringing death and destruction. The lovely, intricate design of a snowflake, if it is multiplied, can be a deadly thing freezing the very life out of a man. The warmth of a summer sun can dry up reservoirs and provide the climate appropriate for riots in the asphalt jungle.

Nor does it mean that a scientist by probing the outer reaches of the immensities of space or by examining the entrails of an atom can discover who and what God is. The world of nature is but the stage on which the drama of life and death is played out. The scientist by dissecting and examining the stage and by rearranging the elements that go into the stage and experimenting with them, cannot possibly discover what the drama is all about.

But it does mean that although the mystery remains, we know that behind all this vast, created world there is a will of love, for we have seen that love came alive for us in a child in a stable and we have seen the depths of that love stretch out its arms on a cross. We may well be baffled and bewildered and driven to distraction at times by the mystery of a world in which there is so much wanton tragedy and suffering—and the mystery remains. We are creatures, not gods. But we are assured that the God behind this mystery is not an impersonal fate, mocking our puny efforts to make sense of it all, but rather that his name is Father.

Moreover, if the creative power which brought into being the world around us has shown us his will and inner nature in Christ, then we also know how this created world is to be used. We have every right as creatures on this earth to probe the atom and explore the outer reaches of space, to devise the wonders of synthetic fabrics and commercial fertilizer, to experiment with test tubes in the effort to find the secrets of life and death, and all the rest of it. For way back in the story of creation it was set down: "Man shall have dominion over all this created world and subdue it." But if Christ is the clue to the heart of the creator God, then we know what the forests and oil reserves and atomic power are to be used for: not to make us fat and wealthy; not even to make us the strongest and richest nation on the face of the earth, for that is not our ultimate destiny; but rather to feed and clothe and house and to provide productive labor for all the sons of men, and especially those who for one reason or another have less than we. Put biblical truth into the practical terms of mid-twentieth-century politics, economics, and international relations, and you see its relevance for foreign aid, conservation programs, and international control of outer space through the United Nations. For if we are assured that God's autograph—the Christ—is written across the very earth we live on and across the infinite galaxies of stars in space, then we have not only the security of knowing that this mysterious place in which we live and move and have our being is a *home,* but also the disturbing knowledge of what all of these riches around us are to be used for.

It all comes down to this: God, the creator of all this incredible vastness which we call the universe, and Christ, the one who comes as a peasant Jewish child and dies at the hands of men like you and me, are one and the same. Whenever we use the word "God" it is filled with all the outgoing love and sacrifice that we associate with the name of Christ; and whenever we use the word "Christ" it is filled with all the majesty and power of the creator of sunsets and galaxies of stars. Think of it! The God who hung out the stars at the beginning of time, who, as the prophet puts it, "calls them all by name," who "thought up" all that scientists are now discovering—and far more than they have ever dreamed of discovering—*this* God comes down to earth in Christ to tell you that he *knows* you, loves you, forgives you all your shabby past, and offers himself to you as your daily companion through all of life's mysterious joys and tragedies, now and forever. We have not done with God or Christ until we can exclaim with the disciples in wonder and awe, "What manner of man is this, that even the winds and the sea obey him!"

Sight for the Blind

He took the Twelve aside and said, "We are now going up to Jerusalem; and all that was written by the prophets will come true for the Son of Man. He will be handed over to the foreign power. He will be mocked, maltreated, and spat upon. They will flog him and kill him. And on the third day he will rise again." But they understood nothing of all this; they did not grasp what he was talking about; its meaning was concealed from them.

As he approached Jericho a blind man sat at the roadside begging. Hearing a crowd going past, he asked what was happening. They told him, "Jesus of Nazareth is passing by." Then he shouted out, "Jesus, Son of David, have pity on me." The people in front told him sharply to hold his tongue; but he called out all the more, "Son of David, have pity on me." Jesus stopped and ordered the man to be brought to him. When he came up he asked him, "What do you want me to do for you?" "Sir, I want my sight back," he answered. Jesus said to him, "Have back your sight; your faith has cured you." He recovered his sight instantly, and he followed Jesus, praising God. And all the people gave praise to God for what they had seen.   *—Luke 18:31-43* (NEB)

As Lent begins you will frequently hear preachers like myself calling Lent a time for self-examination and repentance, a time for deepening our spiritual lives, a time for self-denial and for making sacrifices. But the net result of all this is apt to be confusion worse confounded. For those of us who respond to this call to the observance of Lent immediately start rooting around inside of ourselves to find out what's wrong—as if we didn't know!—throwing ourselves into longer, more frequent, and more self-conscious prayers and devotions; giving up things like candy and movies and cigarettes, denying ourselves a few unnecessary luxuries to make what is called, peculiarly enough, a "self-denial offering." No wonder we get all confused with mixed-up feelings of guilt and self-congratulation struggling for control inside of us. And no wonder we breathe a sigh of relief in six weeks when Easter rolls around and we can finally get some blessed surcease from this strange "deepening of our spiritual lives," which often turns out to be no more than a poking around inside of ourselves looking for some kind of peculiar spiritual enrichment—as if we could manufacture it by a fascination with our innards!

May I suggest an entirely different approach to Lent? That we look not at ourselves at all—at least not primarily—and not first of all certainly, because that's the source of all our confusion and emptiness anyway; but that first of all we look away from ourselves. This approach to Lent is suggested by a passage in the eighteenth chapter of Luke, the story of the healing of blind Bartimaeus.

It begins with Jesus' announcement to his disciples of his coming passion and death, and their bewilderment as a result: "They understood nothing of all this; they did not grasp what he was talking about." Then follows immediately the story of the blind man sitting "by the roadside begging" and "hearing a crowd going past, he asked what was happening." Lent begins with that question: What's happening? What's going on in the world around us? You don't have to root around inside of your spiritual lives to ask that question. All you have to do is to take a look around you to see and hear a profusion of sights and sounds in the world, most of which make very little sense. Watch the struggle that goes on to make a living, or to make a bit more than a living yet without finding satisfaction in the "bit more"; watch the children growing up and moving out only to have their children grow up and move out with few of them really sure why or for what; watch as friends and loved ones face death and move into the unknown darkness; watch the children playing in the streets with balls and dolls one minute only to exchange them before you know it for zip guns and contraceptives; watch successful and unsuccessful men and women divorcing each other and then giving it another try; watch the lines forming at the office of the psychiatrist or the social worker; watch young people crowding into coffee houses to sing their melancholy folk songs while Negroes out in the street sing their melancholy ballad, "We shall overcome some day"; watch the puzzlement of the richest nation on earth wondering what to do with four to five million unemployed and embarrassed by its overflowing wheat bins while Kentucky miners put their children to bed hungry. All I'm saying is that you don't have to pull yourself into all sorts of queer spiritual shapes through "self-examination" to look around and ask the question, "What's happening?" What is going on here? What on earth is God doing in all of this?

The blind man sitting by the roadside of life heard a confusion of noises too, and got his answer: "Jesus of Nazareth is passing by." No sooner had he heard that than he knew exactly what he wanted—his sight. He wanted new eyes. And he received what he wanted at the hands of Jesus of Nazareth: "He recovered his sight instantly; and he followed Jesus, praising God."

This is obviously more than a story of a blind man suddenly able to see faces and trees and colors again. Set against the background of the announcement of the Passion and the disciples' lack of understanding, it is a dramatic exposure of the blindness of the disciples and of the sight that can come to those who would understand "what's happening" in the light of an understanding of the life and death of Jesus of Nazareth passing by. If Lent begins with the question, "What's happening?"—then the next question is what on earth is the significance for all of this of "Jesus of Nazareth passing by"? And we don't get the answer to that question either by rooting around inside ourselves, examining our obvious failures and wringing our hands over them, or by trying desperately to ease the guilt through Lenten "self-denial" offerings of the few pennies a day we might ordinarily spend on desserts or tobacco. We get the answer by looking away from ourselves at Jesus of Nazareth passing by.

The other evening I took another look at Jesus of Nazareth passing by, by reading the Gospel of Luke, the Gospel in which this story appears. May I suggest that instead of reading bits and pieces of the Bible each day in Lent, not a bad habit to get into, of course, it might be far more fruitful to sit down for an hour or two and read one of the Gospels through at one sitting, perhaps using a new and fresh translation, the New English Bible, for example, so that the old story may seem fresh again and also so that you can get a fresh look at the whole story. And then reflect upon it for a day or two.

Two things hit me as I read the whole story in Luke. The first major impression I got—in sharp contrast to the strange noise and confusion in the world around us in which life seems constantly to be hemmed in, restricted, confined, by death and perplexity and tragedy and emptiness and a lack of purpose and meaning—was that here was a man who enlarged the lives of those he touched. New and wonderful things happened. Life began again. Horizons were broadened. The ceiling on life was lifted. From the opening story of the promise of a child to an old and barren woman, Elizabeth, and the child leaping in her womb in the presence of another child in the womb of Mary, on to the closing story of men walking the dusty road to Emmaus, their "hearts on fire" as a stranger talked to them along the way; from beginning to end the Gospel is a story of life being enlarged, broadened, deepened, and heightened. A woman gives her last pittance, all she had in the world, into the temple offering box; a tawdry woman of the streets breaks a box of alabaster ointment, "very precious," over the feet of Jesus; Zacchaeus comes down from a tree to give half his fortune away; a withered hand is restored; demons are expelled from a man crippled and diseased; a woman presses close in the crowd around Jesus and draws health from the hem of his garment. In scene after scene, the dominant impression is that of life enlarged, released, freed from all that hems it in. Even death and darkness cannot write finis to the story of Jesus of Nazareth passing by.

Now it's worth noting that all of this goes on on a tiny, tiny stage. Visitors to the Holy Land never fail to be impressed by the smallness of the stage on which the story of God's invasion of our world took place. The distances are short. Bethlehem, where it all started, is only a few miles from Jerusalem, where it all ended. The whole drama is enacted on a stage no larger than metropolitan New York, all within a radius of about twenty-five miles. So—the enlargement of life that Jesus brings needs no vast panorama, no Hollywood stage setting for a biblical extravaganza. It comes to one man after another where he lives out his ordinary life, in home and shop and street and neighborhood. And is this not important in a world like ours where enlargement has taken place all right, but outside of us rather than within us? It is precisely because of our new awareness of the immensities of space, the possibility of life on other planets, the vast destructive power of the H-bomb now in our hands, the incalculable accumulation of knowledge in recent years, that we feel so insignificant and small and hemmed in. One of the government libraries in Washington contains over one million books and receives seventeen thousand periodicals every month just to keep up with the vast accumulation of knowledge in the field of medicine alone. No wonder that in the face of the enlargement of life around us we feel so lost and unimportant and hemmed in as individuals—as if it didn't matter too much to anyone except for a small circle of friends and relatives whether we lived or died. But the story of Jesus of Nazareth passing by is told on a stage no larger—and no smaller—than the tiny stage on which you and I live out our lives. Can you catch something of the wonder of God's love that he chose to tell his story of the enlargement of life in this way rather than on some huge stage where the individual might feel lost and forgotten?

Read the story of Jesus of Nazareth passing by and see the enlargement of life, the release, the freedom from fear and anxiety and demons and disease. It's like a blind man receiving his sight again. Of a sudden you are grasped by what life might be under God; indeed, by what it can be.

But the enlargement of life is not the only major impression you get from reading Luke's Gospel. The other major impression is that of a life and death conflict. There is an attack going on, and the attack, surprisingly enough, is carried out by this same Jesus of Nazareth. I suppose we're apt to think of the story of Jesus as the story of a man under constant attack and harassment by his enemies and even by his friends who finally caused his suffering and death. It almost makes you feel sorry for him and for God. Poor old God, you know, always on the defensive against the forces of evil, trying so desperately to fight his way out of a jam, like a halfback caught behind the line of scrimmage. Actually the opposite is true. To be sure, he encounters resistance, but the initiative in the drama is always with Jesus of Nazareth. His life and death have been called the "attack of grace."[1] And his weapon is precisely the enlargement of life. The conflict develops as men resist the enlargement of their lives. They don't want it! They'll see him dead first!

So he heals a man on the sabbath day, breaking the

[1] Quoted from Karl Barth in Gerhard Gloege, *The Day of His Coming* (Philadelphia: Fortress, 1963), p. 251.

religious law in the larger interest of mercy. But good religious men are uncomfortable when sacred rules and regulations are broken. So they plan to get rid of him. He sits down to dinner with riffraff, the offscourings of good, decent society; and good, pious men resist the enlargement of love which includes even recognized rascals. He says that a man must give his ultimate allegiance to God if he is to be freed from ultimate allegiance to the power that money brings or to status and the good regard of the neighbors and their standards of behavior, and we all begin to feel uncomfortable, to fidget and hold back and resist *that* kind of enlargement of life!

So the story is the story of resistance to this relentless attack upon our well-cultivated moralities, niceties, pieties, and prejudices, and all the things that hem life in. Until at the end he is left there hanging, alone. And yet, as you read, you are never left with the feeling that the initiative has been taken out of his hands. Even helpless as he is there at the end, nailed fast to the cross beams, his lips can still move: "Father forgive them, for they know not what they do." And you know the initiative, the power, is still in his hands.

And now the meaning of Lent begins to clear up: the shape of the conflict is clarified. God's attack upon the principalities and powers of evil in the world and in ourselves takes the shape of a cross, the shape of suffering love. This is not submission to the evil in the world and in us; this is an offensive weapon, the very power of God at work to bring enlargement, freedom, release to life in the only way that God's power can bring enlargement and defeat the forces that would resist it. For if God were to use his power in any other way, the result would not be enlargement and freedom and release, but the very opposite: denial of freedom, enslavement. We would not even have the power to resist. We would be less than human; and God would be less than God.

This picture of "Jesus of Nazareth passing by" is what the disciples could not and would not understand until it was all over. This was the "sight," the new eyes that were granted to the blind man. And this is the "sight," the new eyes that are offered to our blind eyes too, if we, like blind Bartimaeus, wish it so.

And this is what Lent is for, to take a fresh look at Jesus of Nazareth passing by. And then, after you've taken a good long steady look at the enlargement that he brings and the resistance men offer to it, *then* you can begin to examine yourself—not to discover all those cheap and tawdry failures which make our lives gray and shabby, but to see that all around us God is offering to enlarge our lives, not to free us from the demands of sex or politics or business, of course, but to help us see all of these as potential opportunities for new dimensions of justice and love, broader horizons in opening up the lives of those around us, and to help us see that our "sin" is precisely the resistance we offer to the enlargement of life God would have us know. This is why we examine ourselves, to see this ugly resistance for what it is, the desire to keep our lonely, anxious, fearful little selves, lonely, anxious, fearful, and little. But this would be no more than unhealthy, morbid introspection if we did not examine ourselves constantly in the light of God's attack of grace, his all-out invasion of life here and now with his unconquerable love: even the gates of hell—of death and darkness and fear and loneliness—shall not prevail against it. For Lent without Easter is morbid and pointless. Even death and the gates of hell give in at the last to the relentless attack of grace in Jesus of Nazareth passing by.

"Sight for the blind"—that's what Lent has to offer you, eyes to see a new world around you, new faces in the old, familiar faces you thought you knew so well, eyes to see new openings in the communities in which you live to bring enlargement to the lives of people hemmed in by poverty and injustice and fear and disease and ignorance. And perhaps Lent this year will bring with it new resolve to resist no longer the enlargement, the new dimensions, the broadened horizons, the lifted ceilings in our own lives which God brings to us in the story of Jesus of Nazareth passing by.

Cross and Glory

Now among those who went up to worship at the feast were some Greeks. So these came to Philip, who was from Bethsa'ida in Galilee, and said to him, "Sir, we wish to see Jesus." Philip went and told Andrew; Andrew went with Philip and they told Jesus. And Jesus answered them, "The hour has come for the Son of man to be glorified. Truly, truly, I say to you, unless a grain of wheat falls into the earth and dies, it remains alone; but if it dies, it bears much fruit. He who loves his life loses it, and he who hates his life in this world will keep it for eternal life. If any one serves me, he must follow me; and where I am, there shall my servant be also; if any one serves me, the Father will honor him.
"Now is my soul troubled. And what shall I say, 'Father, save me from this hour'? No, for this purpose I have come to this hour. Father, glorify thy name." Then a voice came from heaven, "I have glorified it, and I will glorify it again."
—*John 12:20-28*

Last fall a sabbatical leave made it possible for us to spend the autumn months in Northern Vermont. People who ought to know called it the drabbest fall in that area that they could remember. And they were right: one cloudy, showery day after another with mud, cold, and snow. The leaves—most of them—simply curled up and turned a drab brown. But every once in a while there came a golden day with bright sun, blue sky, puff clouds, and air like wine, and the remaining spots of color in the foliage glowed brilliantly. On those rare days we experienced what others had described as the "glory of autumn in Vermont."

I suppose most of us think of the "glory of God" in much the same way. For the most part the days and weeks—even years—go by, caught in the dull routine, marked and marred by life's inevitable tragedy, suffering, nagging problems, boredom. And then, perhaps, comes a golden moment, what some like to call a "mountain-top experience," when the "glory of God" shines through.

And the account of God's dealings with men in the Bible would seem to bear this out. For most of those thousand pages we read of trouble and struggle, of rebellion and judgment, and of hopes for a brighter future, punctuated only occasionally by a bush burning but not consumed, a dream of a ladder reaching up to heaven, a breath-taking vision in the temple of the transcendent holiness of God, skies suddenly filled with a chorus of angels at the birth of a child, the moment of transfiguration on a mountain top, the incomprehensible glory of a resurrection. And like the people who lived in those days, we are apt to associate the "glory of God" only with those occasional moments marked by the dazzling brightness appropriate, so we think, to the presence of God.

But this is to misread the Bible, and especially the New Testament. To be sure, "glory" does mean "presence." The "glory of God" means, in effect, the "presence" of God when that presence breaks through to people here on earth. But maybe the reason why we so seldom experience the presence of God, his "glory" here and now, is because we keep looking only for dazzling experiences of the brightness of God's presence. Maybe this is why there is a growing uneasiness today that God is "dead" or at least "absent," that he does not disclose his presence today in the way in which he seemed to make his presence known in biblical times.

But look again at those bright and dazzling moments, particularly in the New Testament, and a strange picture emerges. The presence of God is not located in the brightness of the sky over Bethlehem or in a choir of heavenly angels. The "glory" of which they sang is located precisely in the utter weakness of a freshly-born human child, in human life at its weakest, most defenseless, most helpless moment. Here in a cattle stall, not in the brilliant heavens above, is the "glory," the "presence" of God disclosed.

Or on the Mount of Transfiguration, when our Lord's face shone like the sun and his robes gleamed white as light, the whole scene enveloped in a bright cloud with its mysterious voice, "This is my beloved Son . . ."—even there the "glory," the presence of God, is actually disclosed when Jesus takes Peter and the others and leads them down from the mountain to face an epileptic boy on the plain below. Moreover, you will notice that Jesus told them not to speak of the bright vision or the mysterious voice until after his death and resurrection. In other words, the "glory" was not essentially disclosed in the vision or in the mysterious voice but in his calling as servant to suffer and die. They would not fully understand the bright vision until they had watched him die.

So with the glory of the resurrection. We are apt to forget that the glory of the resurrection was disclosed only to those who had known and followed him as he went about eating with prostitutes and quislings, who had watched him spend his days ministering to the poor, the sick, the dispossessed, who had been with him when he was humiliated, flogged, tried for blasphemy, and executed. The "glory" of the resurrection merely affirms that this is precisely how God looks: a suffering servant of mankind, misunderstood, rejected, crucified. The true "glory" of God —what God really looks like when we peek through the mysterious veil of his holiness to see what lies behind—is most clearly seen in a man suffering and dying on a cross.

So perhaps we can begin to understand what Jesus is talking about when he says, shortly before the end, "Now is my soul troubled. And what shall I say, 'Father, save me from this hour'?" (And the hour was precisely the moment of truth when he entered Jerusalem and faced the inevitable end.) "No," he goes on, "for this purpose I have come to this hour. Father, glorify thy name." And the "name" of the Father is glorified, made evident to those who will see, not in choirs of angels or visions or in a bright, golden sky, but in the moment of brokenness, defeat, and death. The "glory" of God—the presence of God when it is most clearly evident to us on earth—is focused on a man dying on a cross.

Well, what about us? All this was long ago and far away. What about here and now?

Our first reaction—and it's quite natural—is to resist the idea. Like the Jews of old, we think it is a scandal, a stumbling block. And like the Greeks of old, we regard it as foolishness. You can't twist the "glory of God," for heaven's sake, into a sad little scene on a low hill outside of Jerusalem. It doesn't make any sense. And so our natural inclination is to sift out of the meaning of glory that which is more congenial to us, only that which is bright and shining and more obviously triumphant. I suppose that when we speak of the glory of God it's not unlike speaking of the stars and stripes as "old glory": there it is fluttering proudly in the breeze, symbol of our wealth, honor, prestige, and freedom, and the fact that we are thus far, at least, undefeated in war. Can the "glory" of God be anything less?

So, by implication, we sometimes speak of the "glory" of the church, and almost inevitably when it gives evidence of the kind of "glory" most congenial to us: when its buildings are strikingly beautiful or impressive, when the pews are full, the coffers overflowing, when its choirs sound like angels, and when it has sufficient prestige to throw its weight around in the community. And even when we speak of the "glory" of the cross, we prefer to strip it of its broken body, cover it with gleaming silver or brass, and put a spotlight on it so it will shine!

Which is why the church has wisely set apart six weeks in the year, Lent and Holy Week, to make us face up to what the "glory of God," his presence, is really like. Some have suggested the season is far too long and ought to be telescoped. I wonder. Perhaps if all we do in Lent is engage in morbid introspection, in some concentrated navel gazing, wallowing around for forty days in our sins, trying desperately to achieve some kind of repentance, then six weeks *is* far too long. But if the season is used, as it should be, not to keep probing our insides but rather to take a good long steady look at what God is really like—

that his presence on earth, his "glory," comes through most clearly in a servant rejected, humiliated, spit on, broken in death—then I suspect it will take all of six weeks out of the year—and then some!—to overcome our natural resistance to the idea.

So—in the light of the cross and this strange meaning of glory, where can we see God's "glory," his presence at work in the world today? A number of strange and hardly "glorious" pictures come to mind.

There was a minister in Cleveland mightily concerned about the problem of integration in the schools who, while engaging in a public protest, got mangled to death by a bulldozer in the process. A stupid waste, I suppose. Or there's a teacher in a classroom, someone like Sylvia Barrett in *Up the Down Staircase,* who despite all the bureaucratic irritations, defeats, and frustrations, gets a tremendous kick out of seeing to it that her kids learn to read and write and think and develop as persons. Or there's an ordinary house painter who gets tremendous satisfaction out of a job really well done. Or there's a daughter putting up with her elderly, fretful mother who is convinced she has lived too long, as well as an elderly mother putting up with a fretful, impatient daughter. Or there is the student, convinced that the most crucial issue of our times is civil rights, going off to help in voter registration.

Don't misunderstand. It's not clear-cut, this business of trying to discern the "glory of God" in the world around us. "Now we see in a glass darkly." And very darkly at times. And in that dark glass some see civil rights workers, for example, only as troublemakers, scorning respect for law and order, though they'd do well to recall that good and decent people thought of Jesus in precisely the same way. The glass is dark, just as dark now as it was then when they called Jesus a "blasphemer" and trouble-maker and rejected him out of hand! It's *never* easy to see God at work in the world, to discern his glory, not even in the New Testament! Because his glory never looks the way we think it ought to look. And besides, in every instance we could mention today there are mixed motives, human error, and shortsightedness. The glass is always dark. Even Albert Schweitzer, who seemed so clearly to reflect the "glory of God" as a man dedicated to the welfare of the dispossessed, had his critics. It's never clear-cut, the reflected "glory of God" in life today.

But this much is clear. If glory and cross are held together as they are in the New Testament, then whenever —despite mixed motives, despite the risks and the tangled web of good and evil—whenever there is suffering for others, concern for the dispossessed and the unlovely, living primarily for the good of others, there does the "glory of God," his very presence, shine through—however brokenly—in the baffling mishmash of life around us.

Of course it may be that God will grant even to us, occasionally, something more perhaps, glimpses of the "brightness of his glory" too, moments of reassurance, when the sky lights up and angels sing, like the "glory of autumn in Vermont." But this is not the place to *look* for his "glory." These are the glorious moments of assurance which may come to us now and then, but only *after* we have recognized the "glory of God," his vivid presence, in the man suffering for others in the hour when he faces defeat and humiliation and death.

Listen again to him as he prays before being hung on a cross: "Now is my soul troubled. And what shall I say, 'Father, save me from this hour'? No, for this purpose"— precisely to glorify God—"I have come to this hour. Father, glorify thy name."

God's Surprises

And when they drew near to Jerusalem and came to Beth'phage, to the Mount of Olives, then Jesus sent two disciples, saying to them, "Go into the village opposite you, and immediately you will find an ass tied, and a colt with her; untie them and bring them to me. If any one says anything to you, you shall say, 'The Lord has need of them,' and he will send them immediately." This took place to fulfil what was spoken by the prophet, saying,

> "Tell the daughter of Zion,
> Behold, your king is coming to you,
> humble, and mounted on an ass,
> and on a colt, the foal of an ass."

The disciples went and did as Jesus had directed them; they brought the ass and the colt, and put their garments on them, and he sat thereon. Most of the crowd spread their garments on the road, and others cut branches from the trees and spread them on the road. And the crowds that went before him and that followed him shouted, "Hosanna to the Son of David! Blessed be he who comes in the name of the Lord! Hosanna in the highest!" —*Matthew 21:1-9*

One of the most embarrassing questions raised by the New Testament is to ask what actually happens to all the splendid promises it holds out to us: peace, joy, and the abundant life. For the New Testament is not at all squeamish about talking about fulfillment and rewards. But where in the world are they?

72

You look around at the lives of the more prominent Christians in years past or today and you begin to wonder. Peace, for example, turns out for Paul to be years of constant conflict and sleepless nights ending in a Roman prison; and for Father Damien a lingering, horrible death from leprosy in a leper colony. Joy turns out for Peter to be a crucifixion and for Dietrich Bonhoeffer execution by the Nazis. Abundant life turns out for Stephen to be a lynch mob with stones instead of a rope, for Helen Keller a lifetime of silence and darkness, for Medgar Evers a bullet in the back. What shall we make of it? We are asked to die with Christ that we may rise with him to newness of life. And all that happens, apparently, is that we die with him.

Does it mean that all of these glorious promises dangled before our eyes are illusions so far as this life is concerned, held up in front of us to keep us muddling through disease and poverty and injustice and boredom and atomic chaos, "pie in the sky" not to be realized here and now but "by and by" in some possible afterlife, if then? But if Christ is to be trusted, this is not so. To be sure, the promises of God are not limited to this world of time and space, but peace and joy and the abundant life are to be found here and now too. At least so we are led to believe. But when and where do they come true? Why is it these glowing promises turn out so often to be dust and ashes in our mouths?

The Palm Sunday story, the triumphal entry of Christ into Jerusalem with the palms and hosannas, can give us an opportunity to face this whole embarrassing problem

73

of promise, fulfillment, and reward and possibly offer some clues as to an answer.

To begin with, there is a sense in which the whole Old Testament comes to its climax right here in the Palm Sunday story. For we cannot begin to understand the lights and shadows, the intriguing paradox of this strange and fascinating story, the right cheers for the right person for the wrong reasons, without some understanding of what the Old Testament is all about. One of our biggest problems today is to try to understand the Christian faith—the New Testament—without knowing much if anything about the Old Testament except a miscellaneous and disjointed collection of Bible stories: Cain and Abel, Noah and the ark, Joseph and his coat of many colors, Jonah and the whale, together with a smattering of the prophets and a selection or two from the Psalms. Yet to try to understand the New Testament apart from what went before is like trying to make sense out of the current struggle for civil rights without a knowledge of the slave trade, the Civil War, and the painful period of reconstruction which followed.

For what we have here in the Old Testament is a long and fascinating history of this very problem: the glowing promises of God and the constant disillusionment when the fulfillment failed to live up to the promises. The heaven-sent manna in the wilderness turned bitter and sour, not nearly so tasty as the leeks and garlic they'd had in Egypt. The promise of a "land flowing with milk and honey" turned out to be no heaven on earth at all, but a place where a man had to work and sweat and fight for a living. Not only so, but the promised land was sacked and plundered and the people carted off into exile. Then in exile in Babylon came the magnificent promise of freedom and Jerusalem miraculously restored—a new age—with peace and justice and all the nations of the earth streaming toward the Holy City to worship the God of Abraham, Isaac, and Jacob. And what did that glowing promise turn out to be but a dreary trek back across the hot sands of the desert to a city destroyed and a temple in ruins and the tears and sweat which went into rebuilding, only to see the city, the land, and the people conquered by one nation after another. Meanwhile, the promise kept luring them on: This time it was to be a Messiah King, God's own emissary, who, after all these disappointments and disillusionments, would establish once and for all the new age—a veritable heaven on earth—and who in his own person would fulfill all the frustrated hopes and promises of God for his people: peace, joy, and the abundant life.

And on Palm Sunday he came! The crowds recognized him. The promised king, just as the prophet had said, "Humble and riding upon an ass, on a colt, the foal of an ass." All the hopes and dreams and promises of God of a thousand years and more of frustration and disillusionment were centered in that one man leading this strange procession into the Holy City: "Hosanna to the Son of David! Blessed is he that cometh in the name of the Lord!"

But by Friday morning the bubble had burst. Once again the all too familiar taste of dust and ashes in the mouth, and they spit it out in a fury: "Crucify! We have no king but Caesar!"

This is not just ancient history. This is an accurate picture of why the promises of God so often turn out to be dust and ashes in our mouths too. Why? For one thing, the people back there in Jerusalem had so distorted and twisted the meaning of God's promises into what they wanted God's promises to look like that they could not recognize the fulfillment when it came. Hence the dust and ashes.

It's not unlike a starry-eyed young couple getting married with the promise of "living happily ever after" ringing in their ears. Then comes the fulfillment of the promise: hair curlers and stubby beards, the maddening crunch of toast between the teeth of the beloved across the breakfast table, the short tempers and clash of wills and personalities and the inevitable compromises until suddenly the realization comes that if this is what "living happily ever after" means, they'll have none of it, and before long it's the dust and ashes of the divorce court. Just so with the crowd in Jerusalem. If this poor rabbi crowned with thorns, the helpless victim of cheap politicians and scheming priests, the butt of stupid jokes by clumsy soldiers . . . if this is the fulfillment of a thousand years of divine promises, then they will have none of it. "His blood be on us and on our children."

And we are the children. And we're not so very different. If "peace" means added tensions and sleepless nights and involvement in the complex and overwhelming problems of our times; if "joy" means pain and bereavement; if the "abundant life" means years of loneliness with no children running around the house, or carrying a crippling disease around all the days of your life, or standing in line looking for a job or for unemployment compensation, then we're apt to look elsewhere too. You see, we want God's promises to look the way we want them to look. And if that's the way it is with us, then God's promises will always turn to dust and ashes in our mouths too.

A popular misunderstanding of the Jerusalem crowd on Palm Sunday is to call it fickle: "hosanna," one day; "crucify," the next. But the crowd wasn't fickle. It was frighteningly consistent. The fulfillment of the promise did not match the expectation. Hence, quite consistently, the cry changed from, "Blessed is he that cometh," to "crucify."

All of which underlines the fact that the fulfillment always involves suffering and death. So Paul: "If we have died with Christ, we believe that we shall also rise with him to newness of life." And so one of our embarrassments concerning the New Testament emphasis upon reward is undercut. The reward is not cheap. The fulfillment never looks like fulfillment when we are faced with the reality of the choice before us.

The struggle for civil rights is a case in point. No one in America today—or very few, at least—does not want the fulfillment of the promise lodged in our heritage: a life of peace and justice and freedom for all where everyone, regardless of race, color, or creed, has equal opportunity to make of his life what he will. But a large, bitter segment in America—which includes most of us at one time or another—is unwilling to accept the fulfillment of the promise on the terms of death to a way of life which denies the fulfillment of the promise. So they sing their hosannas on July 4 in praise of the Declaration of Independence and the Constitution, but cry "crucify" when the fulfillment means death to their way of life in segregated schools, labor unions, suburbs, summer resorts, motels, to say nothing of churches.

But even if we are willing to endure death to our deep-rooted prejudices, there is no guarantee that the fulfillment will be automatic or that it will match our expectations. Some of the volunteers in the Peace Corps report the deep disillusionment which comes with the recognition that the problems in the world where they serve are so vast and complex and overwhelming that the tiny pittance one individual can offer seems to be swallowed up and lost in the hopelessness and ambiguities in the situation. The promise that "he who loses his life for my sake shall find it" may not be immediately apparent. We are thrown back to a radical trust in God and his way of love on a cross, reduced to the sheer, raw courage to accept the fact that my thoughts are not his thoughts, neither are his ways my ways.

Those who choose to die with him on Good Friday cannot know beforehand what the fulfillment will be like. The reward does not turn out to be an easy *quid pro quo* after all. We have to take his promises on his terms and let God be God.

But there's another problem. Even if we are willing to take God's promises on his terms, there's always the danger that we'll expect the fulfillment to be a stereotype: the same for me as for everybody else. And it's not strange that this should be so. For here in America the promise of the abundant life has a sameness about it that's almost terrifying. For what is the dream for the future for most Americans? After an early struggle to get started, a possible hitch in the army, making your way in a job, preferably in the security of a big corporation or big government or a big university, to the place where you can start a family and buy or rent a modest home, then the fulfillment: a lovely suburban home with two cars, a stereo with a knowledgeable collection of records, an outdoor fireplace and swimming pool, a golf club nearby, music lessons for the kids, a covey of friends, a bundle of stocks to see the children through college and a little extra salted away for retirement. The same for everybody.

Is it any wonder that preachers like myself fall into the pattern and lead you to expect that peace and joy and the abundant life are just as stereotyped—the same for everybody? And the picture we give you of the Christian man on whom God has showered his blessings, for whom all God's promises for this life have come true, often enough looks for all the world like a pious advertisement of happy, American suburban living: A well-scrubbed family, shorn of all bad habits like smoking and drinking, smiling happily and healthily, Bibles in their hands, marching off to church, their eyes lifted confidently to the cross atop the neighboring spire.

And yet how differently God works! Just because he insists on treating each one of us as an individual and in the light of our own individual needs and possibilities. So that what may be joy for one may not be joy for another.

Here, for example, is a shy, mousy little woman, a devoted Christian, who finds her peace and joy and abundant life in service within a confined little cosmos, her family, her neighborhood, and her parish church. And yet another equally devoted Christian might find her peace and joy a veritable hell of mediocrity and passivity or both.

For he finds his peace and joy in taking obvious risks, in throwing himself into the middle of the battle for integration, in trying to solve the big and complex problems of love and justice in a loveless society. And yet still a third equally devoted Christian would be appalled both by the mousy little woman and the energetic activist. For he finds his peace and joy in solitary creativity, in writing or painting or music or architecture, to express through the arts something of what he knows and feels of the beauty and tragedy and drama of life under God. And so we could go on.

For each the promise is the same: peace, joy, and abundant life; and each life reflects the same love; but love is indeed a "many-splendored thing." For each the same promise and yet for each how differently it works out; and how unsatisfying for one the specific fulfillment of the promise would be for any of the others.

Maybe all we can say to any individual is, "You'll be surprised." And that's why this may possibly be the most unsatisfying sermon you've ever read. For the fulfillment of God's glowing promises is certainly never going to turn out to be precisely what we would like it to be because "my thoughts are not your thoughts, neither are your ways my ways, saith the Lord." Nor is the fulfillment going to be the same in my life as in yours. God's blessings, fortunately, have not succumbed to the processing and packaging of the supermarket: the same frozen cauliflower for everybody.

And how wonderful that it should be so. For we live by faith and to live by faith is to let God be God. To know in advance precisely what God's promises will be like is to make of God's promises an embarrassment, and of God no God at all but the proprietor of a coupon store where you cash in the books of green stamps—your devotion and obedience and faith—for the promised premiums in the catalogue, the same premiums for everybody, of course. God is faithful to his promises of peace and joy and the abundant life, but the fulfillment of his promises will be as surprising in your life as it will be in mine. "Eye hath not seen, nor ear heard, neither have entered into the heart of man, the things which God hath prepared for them that love him." And blessed is the man who, unlike the Jerusalem crowd, can recognize the fulfillment of the promise when it comes!

Disturbed by Joy

At the conclusion of a three-hour service on Good Friday, the host minister bade me goodbye: "I hope you have a blessed Easter." It was a natural thing to say. I think it was not just pious language; I think he meant it. And so do others who say it in more conventional terms, "Have a happy Easter." For this is the normal expectation for this day of days, isn't it so? That it will be marked by joy. This is its dominant mood: the joyful celebration of victory over the suffering and death and darkness of Good Friday.

But it's a strange circumstance that in the narrative accounts of the resurrection, joy was not the initial reaction. The initial reaction was one of embarrassment, of fear, of awe.

I know it is always a ticklish business to attempt to get back of the Easter message itself, "That Christ died . . . that he was buried and that he was raised on the third day . . . ," and attempt to discover what actually happened through a study of the resurrection narratives. It's ticklish because even the least scholarly among us can recognize through the most casual reading of the narratives in the four Gospels that they do not agree in detail as to how this experience of Christ alive first came, or even as to where.

Furthermore, it is generally acknowledged that the narratives which describe the resurrection appearances are considerably later than the record of the content of the message itself. And, as scholars suggest, the narratives may well be embroidered by legendary additions.

And yet, granting all this, it is still a curious fact that in all four accounts it is clear that the immediate impact of the experience of Christ alive is not joy, as we might well expect. Rather it is an experience of embarrassment, of fear, almost of terror. So the New English Bible in its translation of the Easter narratives uses words like "terrified," "dumbfounded," "beside themselves with terror," "falling prostrate before him." Even Günther Bornkamm, who comes right out and says that the story of the women at the tomb in Mark is "obviously a legend," nevertheless exclaims, "(But see) how his story is told! The wonderful event of the resurrection is not even depicted, such is the reticence and awe."[1] And when you come to the account in the Gospel of John, in its way it is even more reticent. It says simply, "They did not recognize him."

Now all this adds up to the fact that whatever else the disciples and followers of Jesus may have hoped for, desired, anticipated, prior to the death and after it, quite unlike our attitude today, they did not expect this! This, apparently, was the last thing they expected. They were embarrassed, frightened, confused, awe-struck. And it seems to me, if we are to recapture the authentic message of Easter, its substance, we have to come to terms with this strange reaction.

And yet, admittedly, it is all but impossible for us to

[1] Günther Bornkamm, *Jesus of Nazareth* (New York: Harper, 1960), p. 183.

recapture the same mood of embarrassment and fright. Easter is hardly surprising or embarrassing for most of us. All through Lent and Holy Week and Good Friday, we anticipate its joy—as we should! We'd be playing a morbid game of charades if we didn't. And so each year we anticipate reliving the joy that it brings. Even now we look forward to the next Easter, hoping that it will be late. Because, despite the obvious distortions of the resurrection message in the analogy of the renewal of nature in the Spring, we've come to expect nature to join in the joyous celebration. The crocus and the daffodil ought to be nodding their silent hallelujahs too. But in all of this annual anticipation, this looking forward to the expected joy of Easter, something tends to drop out of our understanding of the substance of the Easter message.

Moreover, this lack of embarrassment and surprise is fed by the old Platonic notion of the immortality of the soul. We know that it is theologically disreputable these days to assume that there is some indestructible inner core inside of us which death cannot touch, which makes its claim on God to see to it that when we die we really don't. But it's difficult to shake off. We may reject it with our minds, but we've taken it in with our mother's milk, our culture is filled with hints of it, and it dies hard. Yet as long as it persists there's not much embarrassment when Easter rolls around with its announcement that what we've felt all along to be true is now given its annual Christian sanction. Death cannot be the end, Easter or no Easter.

But if all our normal expectations regarding Easter undercut and contradict this strange reaction of embarrassment and fear on that first Easter morning, a radically different mood works powerfully against it too. And that is the prevailing mood that the resurrection as a happy ending spoils the whole story, that the drama of Jesus would be far stronger and make a far greater appeal to this post-Christian age without all this supernatural clap-trap brought in at the end with a dead man suddenly brought back to life again. Wouldn't the story of Jesus of Nazareth be more powerful and truer to itself in being less self-centered, if his life had ended in death? How much more courageous were he to give his life in obedient trust to the God who made him and gave him his mission without this "reward" tacked on at the end. Some people say they'll take their Christianity straight, thank you, without any Hollywood ending which leaves everyone living happily ever after.

It's an understandable reaction, this mood which rejects the resurrection stories as pious fiction. The only trouble with it, apart from the fact that it denies the sum and substance of the earliest Christian records we have, is that it disregards entirely this strange reaction in the Easter narratives. When they experienced Christ alive they didn't go walking off hand in hand into the sunset with a choir of angels singing softly in the wings, "There is a happy land. . . ." On the contrary, "They were terrified . . . dumbfounded . . . ran away beside themselves with terror."

Although it is impossible for us to recapture this mood after all the years, perhaps if we can come to some understanding of what lay behind it and why it persists in all the resurrection narratives, it may give added depth to our appreciation of the substance of the Easter message, that Christ died and rose again.

For what it means, to begin with, is that we cannot escape God—even in death. May not the resistance to the miracle of the resurrection uncover a deep-seated desire not to let go of my hold on life—even in death? For if death is the end, if there is nothing more, then I through my mortal body rotting in the grave have the last word, not God. Then God and his ways, which are not *our* ways, are made to coincide with my understanding of courage and faithfulness and reward. For all the honesty evident in the refusal to accept the miraculous, the supernatural here at the end of Christ's life, is there not imbedded in that honest reluctance a trace at least of the pride of the creature who insists on determining life's ultimate destiny rather than leaving the issue to God? I will trust God in life here and now, give myself wholly to his will of love here and now, even grant him the power to bring about a new life—a "new being"—here and now, but I will not grant him power over my death.

But beyond that, does not the resurrection mean that we cannot escape the startling ways in which God acts? Obviously the disciples, the women, the followers of Jesus, were distraught and disillusioned in the face of his death. They wept at the cross and on the way to the tomb. But they had accepted it. They had come to terms with it. "They went with their spices to anoint him." How that little detail underlines how quickly they learned to accept Christ's death and live with it. For does not all life end so? You and I quickly learn to come to terms with grief and disillusionment and death. We learn to live with it. We have to.

So was not part of their astonishment and embarrassment and fear the sudden realization that God would act *through* suffering and disillusionment and death? To be sure they'd had their hopes, their dreams, all the promises of life abundant which he had held out to them. But never in their wildest moments had they considered the possibility that God would accomplish his vast purposes of love *through* death and suffering and disillusionment. It's one thing to come to terms with death and disillusionment, to live with it and accept it. We all have to do that. It's quite another to be faced with the reality that this is how God acts, how he works out his purposes for the world. No wonder they were dumbfounded and terrified. For now they knew. God does not save us from suffering and death; he saves us through it. "Take up your cross and follow me" was no longer a possibility to be held at arm's length as a conceivable course of action alongside some others perhaps less stringent. Now it was there, living before their eyes. Life—abundant life—is not cheap.

And that brings us to this: before Easter brings its inevitable joy, it brings judgment. And no doubt that's what terrified them too. For as they buried him in the tomb, they buried not only their hopes and dreams and all the promises he had held out to them, all the love and care he had shown, all his concern for the unlovely and downtrodden—all this was buried with him. But this was not all that was buried. Along with all this they also buried their shoddy faith, their shabby quarrels as to who was to be greatest in the kingdom, all the petty jealousies and impatience with him, the ugly scenes of denial and betrayal—all this was buried with him too. And in that burial, as Tillich has reminded us, is the powerful symbol of being forgotten.[2] As they buried him, they also buried the fact that they all forsook him and fled in the not unreasonable hope that that unpleasantness would soon be forgotten too.

No wonder they were "beside themselves with terror" on that first resurrection morning. For all of this was now alive again! The promises, the love, the vibrant life they had known, to be sure, but all the sad betrayals and shabby pettiness and indifference too. It had all come back! For there is no forgetting. Now it is all alive again. "And they were afraid." Is it surprising? Death was no longer a forgetting; it was a remembering.

And so the most characteristic initial word on Easter is not, "Be of good cheer," but, "Be not afraid." For the one who returns, who brings it all back to life again, who permits no escape into death, who allows no burial, no forgetting, is the one we know. And with recognition, the fear, the embarrassment, turns into joy: "Then were the disciples glad when they saw the Lord." For now despite the judgment, the bringing alive of all he had been and of all they had been, they knew they could trust that the judgment he brought alive was the judgment of love. So Easter becomes a commentary on John's words, "There is no fear in love, for perfect love casteth out fear."

Now, is this gladness, this joy, possible until the last enemy, death, has actually been overcome? Not just for ourselves but for others? There are those who say, as one college chaplain said to me not long ago, that the meaning of Easter is primarily the reality of the new life Christ

[2] Paul Tillich, *The Eternal Now* (New York: Scribner, 1963), p. 33.

brings here and now; what happens to us afterward is secondary. And there's much to be said for that, of course. For it's true, what God has to offer to us now through the life, death, and resurrection of Christ is the conquest of all life's enemies in the world around us: the injustice and prejudice and indifference and fascination with ourselves, the anxieties and resulting pride and self-justification. All of these enemies of life here and now are overcome in the reconciling love of God in Christ. We don't have to run around like scared rabbits—or, perhaps more accurately, like frightened hyenas—bolstering our little insecurities by feeding on the lives of those around us. Life—abundant life—is a possibility for us here and now. All the doors that shut us in here and now, fear and estrangement and hostility, all of these are overcome. The doors are opened to abundant life.

But if death, the last enemy, is not destroyed, the last door not opened, then what is life's issue? Fertilizer for the generations to come? To be sure, Medgar Evers, the little Negro children in Sunday school, and the rest of the martyrs in the civil rights struggle have provided powerful fertilizer not only for sermons but for the civil rights movement. But is the last door, the door that banged shut on them—death—to remain shut? The door which says No to all life's ultimate hopes and dreams?

I can understand a man saying that so far as he's concerned it makes no difference. The door can remain shut since there's so much in life to be realized here and now. But is this not, in the end, at least tainted with a self-centered view? What of the thousands upon thousands of people who have known nothing but closing doors in life here and now: the mentally defective, the deformed children, the warped and twisted minds and bodies that know little if anything in this world but doors banging shut in their faces from childhood on until the last door, the last enemy, bangs shut. What about them? Defective fertilizer, perhaps?

T. S. Eliot puts a haunting line into the mouth of one of the Magi coming to seek the child born in Bethlehem:

> . . . were we led all that way
> for Birth or Death? . . .[3]

No, says Paul. All of life's enemies, including the last enemy, are overcome. "For he must reign until he has put all his enemies under his feet. The last enemy to be destroyed is death. . . . Death is swallowed up in victory."

So the Easter cycle: from death and grief and disillusionment, through embarrassment, fear, and even terror, to the joy that is its ultimate and predominant mood. For God's Yes will not abide life's No or death's No. "Thanks be to God who giveth us the victory through our Lord Jesus Christ."

[3] T. S. Eliot, "Journey of the Magi," *Collected Poems, 1909-1962* (New York: Harcourt, Brace & World, Inc., 1963), p. 69. Used by permission.

The Final Horizon

No doubt when you've been driving along in a car, especially in rolling country, you've played the same sort of little game with yourself that I have. As you come up over a rise or around a bend in the road, you've made a brief mental note of the next horizon—another hill or bend in the road—and then gone back to enjoying the more immediate sights along the way. And then when that horizon has been reached, the process is repeated. The trip becomes in a very quiet and almost subconscious way the conquest of one horizon after another.

We do the same sort of thing far more consciously and definitely as we move along the road of life. For life is a succession of horizons, some near—some far. And the conscious recognition of them helps make the intervening time more meaningful. The immediate horizon may be simply dinner time tonight with certain specific tasks to be done meanwhile. Or for those raising a family there's a more distant horizon, the day when the youngsters will have flown the coop and established homes for themselves. Meanwhile we tangle with the problems of educating and preparing them for that day, knowing that there will come an end to it.

All this, of course, is little more than common sense. It's this conscious recognition of horizons in life which helps make meaningful and significant the immediate tasks at hand. But what about life's final horizon? It's rare these days that a person takes the same common-sense, conscious attitude toward the final horizon, the fact that one day he will die.

Some time ago an intriguing little story appeared in *The New Yorker.* It was the story of a man on his way home from the office on a rainy Friday evening to face a cluster of minor problems involving the various members of his family. Among them: a teen-age son who'd taken the car without permission and banged it up, a wife suddenly panicked by imaginary symptoms occasioned by an article on pernicious anemia she had picked up and read at her hairdresser's a day or so before, and a father who was getting too old to live as he wanted to live, alone in his own large house. The problems were minor and familiar. He had handled them all before in the same easy way, from the expected lecture to his son and jocular reassurance to his wife to the customary talk with his father about the advantages of a small, bright apartment. But on that rainy Friday evening, as he made his way home through mid-Manhattan, he happened to see a man who had just been run down by a car, lying dead in the middle of the street. And for only the second or third time in his life, the final horizon which, of course, had always lurked in the background, shadowy and almost unreal, came sharply into focus. The conscious realization that he too was going to die one day hit him like a sledge hammer. It made a difference when he got home that night. The lecture to his son came out as expected but it seemed unreal and inconsequential, as if he were not really talking

with his son. Nor could he summon up the expected ban-
tering tone with his wife to reassure her that she was
plagued with imaginary demons. He tried, but it didn't
come off. When he got around to his father he gave up
and simply told him that if he wanted to live in his own
big house there was no good reason why he shouldn't.
The story goes on to indicate the subtle changes that went
on in the lives of the family as a result of the sudden recognition in this man's life of the final horizon.

But the point of the story is not simply the fact that
changes occurred in these lives as a result of the sudden,
open recognition of death, but that the author had to use
the rather drastic device of dramatic coincidence—a fatal
street accident at the precise moment this man was leaving his office—to bring the point home, and also that *The
New Yorker* thought the theme unusual enough to war-
rant publication.

The New Yorker was right, of course. One of the
striking characteristics of our time is the absurd lengths to
which we go to keep death out of sight and out of mind.
There was a healthier and brighter day when death, along
with the other basic facts of life like birth, marriage, bearing children, and raising a family, was openly accepted as
an integral part of life. The burial ground surrounding
the church, for example, stood in the center of the community. It was there, and it was foolish and unnatural
to try to avoid it. Moreover a man was buried from the
church, the same place where he was baptized and married
and sat with his children of a Sunday morning. Today we
hide our burial grounds on the outskirts of the town where
we rarely have to see them. And if we can't actually hide

them, we try to hide them behind euphemisms like "Memorial Park" so that the name, at least, will not carry with it too strong an odor of death. Moreover, today, a man is usually buried from a funeral home. This is curious! It's a place which is used for no other purpose and where we never enter except at the time of death. It's as if there were a conspiracy to put death into parentheses.

It is reported that William Randolph Hearst who accumulated vast power and wealth in his lifetime would never allow anyone to use the word death in his presence. Much in our life today expresses the same taboo. We frankly and openly take into account every other horizon except the last. And as a result there is an underlying anxiety which infects our lives, a nameless dread which often enough never even rises to the surface to be recognized for what it is until, perhaps, you happen to run across a man lying dead on the street of a rainy Friday evening.

Please do not misunderstand. The intention here is not to be morbid. It is quite the opposite. If there is anything morbid about death it arises out of the refusal to face it and take it into account. The Christian faith is not morbid when it takes death frankly and openly into account. The Christian year provides several festivals when we are asked to face up to the fact of death. All Saints' Day, for example, is one of them. It's a day when we recall not only those of the faith who have lived and died and now live on eternally, "a great multitude which no man could number, of all nations and kindreds and peoples and tongues standing before the throne . . ."; it's also a day when we recall that we too shall one day face the final horizon. So it is, too, with Easter and the Easter season. As a matter of fact, for the Christian every day in the year is bathed in the victorious glow of the resurrection from the dead. Every Sunday—the first day in the week—is a celebration of that victory over death. But the victory is not a hollow one. Jesus did not just go on living after he was crucified. He died—body, soul, all of him! The final horizon had come for him just as it comes to all of us. And it is only as we face the fact that death, the last enemy, had come that the Easter joy can mean anything; that the last enemy had been conquered; that God had raised him up from death to life again; that the final horizon had been overcome.

There is a healthy realism about the Bible. It doesn't hide from any of the facts of life. It looks every single one of them squarely in the eye, takes them all into account—sin, death, suffering—and then announces triumphantly, the Lord God omnipotent reigneth! Which is why, contrary to what a lot of people seem to believe, the earliest Christians did not go around talking about what a wonderful and unselfish life this Jesus of Nazareth lived before he died. The earliest sermons did not content themselves with exhortations to live the Sermon on the Mount and practice the golden rule and try to live as Christ lived, like so many sermons today. No. The record is perfectly clear on this. The earliest Christian sermons announced the victory of the resurrection over death. They were realists. There was no sense in telling people to live good lives and love their neighbors until the lurking anxiety in every man's life—death—had been brought out into the open and dealt with.

Now, does this clear-eyed realism make any practical difference? Suppose, instead of constantly pushing the thought of the final horizon into the background and attempting to avoid it as much as possible, it is brought frankly into the picture and taken into account, what difference does it make?

It will make at least one big difference for our inner serenity of mind, what Paul calls the "peace of God." This is not a superficial peace of mind, the kind we get on a satisfying vacation, for example, when we get away from the tensions and surface anxieties of life and enjoy the peace and quiet of Florida or California sunshine in the winter, or the mountains in Vermont, or a lake in upper Minnesota in the summer. There is much to be said for this kind of refreshment. But it is temporary. And sometimes it only serves to underline the deeper tensions and anxieties of the rest of the year, until we wish we could get away from it all all the time instead of for just a few weeks.

There is a deeper serenity which comes to the man who takes death into account. For one of the deep causes of our anxiety is the constant fear of being "found out." Every day of our lives records the little deceptions by which we try to hide what we really are from the world, from our friends, from our families, and even from ourselves. Sometimes these little deceptions are perfectly innocent, like a woman using lipstick, because everyone recognizes the deception for what it is. More frequently, however, they may be dangerous, even poisonous. It's amazing, for example, how much of our time is spent simply justifying ourselves and our actions and even our motives to others and to ourselves. A wife will dream up ingenious excuses to justify her little shopping extravagances, particularly if they were "bargains." The husband will do the same to justify himself for spending so little time with the children. Or crack open a discussion which has drifted into argument and from argument into an ugly, bitter quarrel, and almost invariably you will find the cause for the bitterness has been this consuming urge to justify ourselves, to prove ourselves to be "right." We are consumed by the desire to appear to be "right" whereas we know, deep within ourselves, that we are not "right," that no judgment, no motive of ours is pure and unmixed. So we go on, day after day, hiding behind our deceptions, justifying ourselves, fearful that even those we love, our wives and children, will find out what we're really like inside.

Now, if at the end of the road, when we reach the final horizon, there is nothing but the bare fact that we *will* be "found out," that we shall stand in the face of him "from whom no secrets are hid," is it surprising that we try to banish the thought—hide our cemeteries, get funerals out of church into funeral homes, and place a taboo on the word "death"?

The Christian, however, knows an inner serenity. He takes death and this business of being "found out" (which is what judgment really means) into account, brings it out into the open and into the present tense. For the God who will face him *then* at the end of the road, when he will be seen without any pretense or defense, sees him *now* for what he really is and accepts him (which is what forgiveness really means). And what a relief that is here and now, to know that there is one who sees us just as we are, who sees us as we are unwilling for anyone else to see us, in a way we are unwilling even to see ourselves, and accepts us! Then the silly pretensions, this futile business of constantly trying to justify ourselves, are seen for what *they* are, and we can accept ourselves because God sees us and accepts us just as we are. Such an inner serenity—the very peace of God—makes it possible for us to handle the surface tensions and anxieties of life because the deeper anxiety has been resolved through accepting God's love and forgiveness.

The Christian life might well be described as the art of living with death. And there is no completely satisfying way of life apart from that. So Paul can write exultingly about life here and now, "We are more than conquerors," because he has also been persuaded that death—the last enemy— has been taken into account and conquered. The result in your life and mine may very well be an increased aliveness such as Edna St. Vincent Millay describes:

> Ah, up from the ground sprang I
> and hailed the earth with such a cry
> As is not heard save from a man
> Who has been dead and lives again.[1]

[1] From "Renascence." From *Collected Poems*, Harper and Row. Copyright 1912, 1940 by Edna St. Vincent Millay. Used by permission.

Tell Me Thy Name!

The same night he arose and took his two wives, his two maids, and his eleven children, and crossed the ford of the Jabbok. He took them and sent them across the stream, and likewise everything that he had. And Jacob was left alone; and a man wrestled with him until the breaking of the day. When the man saw that he did not prevail against Jacob, he touched the hollow of his thigh; and Jacob's thigh was put out of joint as he wrestled with him. Then he said, "Let me go, for the day is breaking." But Jacob said, "I will not let you go, unless you bless me." And he said to him, "What is your name?" And he said, "Jacob." Then he said, "Your name shall no more be called Jacob, but Israel, for you have striven with God and with men, and have prevailed." Then Jacob asked him, "Tell me, I pray, your name." But he said, "Why is it that you ask my name?" And there he blessed him. So Jacob called the name of the place Peni'el, saying, "For I have seen God face to face, and yet my life is preserved." —*Genesis 32:22-30*

Today the church celebrates the name of God, a rather cumbersome and forbidding name, what James Stewart has called the "strong name of the Trinity," Father, Son, and Holy Spirit. But that's pretty complicated, isn't it? And what's in a name anyway? Not much these days.

Sometimes we sit around chuckling over the ancient meanings given to the names we bear. My name happens to be Edmund, which means defender of property, a ridiculous name for a preacher without an acre or a lot to his name. George means farmer. Roy means king. And Hannah means grace. My father hit the *New York Times* some years ago when in a sermon he parodied a popular song, "Yes, we have no more Hannahs." For there are fashions in names as in hats. Susan and Jennifer and Sandra are more popular today than Phoebe, Miranda, or Hannah. But only because of sound or fashion, not because Susan means lily and Phoebe means shining.

It was not always so. There was a time when a name was the clue to the very nature of a man. Jacob meant supplanter and Jesus or Joshua meant saviour or deliverer. And if a man knew the name of his god, he held the very secret to his nature and power.

All of which brings me to a story back in that shadowy area of the Old Testament where saga, legend, poetry, and history all blend together into the dramatic and unforgettable stories of the patriarchs. It's a weird and eerie story of a man who crossed a river in the dead of night and was seized by a river demon. They struggled in the darkness, thrashing about in the icy water, until at length the man cried, "Tell me thy name!" It was shrewd strategy. For if he could learn the name of the demon, he'd hold the secret to his power; he could escape. But the demon was crafty too, and refused to reveal his identity.

So much of the story, at least, is legend. But out of that legend has come one of the great stories of Jacob. A story that is not just Jacob's story, but everyman's. It's your story and mine, that weird and eerie struggle in the dark with some nameless deity. It may, indeed, be the story of these days in which we live.

Jacob, like so many of us, was a religious man in his fashion. And he was also no fool in the ways of the world. Shrewd and crafty, he'd outsmarted his dull-witted brother, Esau, and tricked him into selling his birthright for a mess of pottage. Then, aided and abetted by his equally crafty mother, Rebecca, he'd cheated Esau out of his aging father's blessing by covering his arms and hands with goatskins. Esau may not have been very bright but he had a temper, and in a rage he threatened Jacob's life. So Jacob took to his heels.

But all that was twenty years ago and now Jacob, at long last, was going home again for the first time. It was night on the banks of the river Jabbok and tomorrow Jacob would have to face Esau. Would Esau let bygones be bygones or would he carry out his twenty-year-old threat? Anxious, fearful of what tomorrow might bring, Jacob was alone. It was as if his whole past had caught up with him that dark night. He remembered not only the trickery he'd used on Esau but also the dazzling vision of a ladder reaching up to heaven. He remembered the nights he'd prayed and the days he'd lived by his wits. Like most of us, Jacob was a puzzling mixture: a man of God and a man of the world, a hardworking man devoted to his wife and children but, when the chips were down, not averse to using whatever means were at hand—even God—to achieve his ends. But now it was night. And tomorrow there was Esau.

And so, plagued with memories and trembling for what tomorrow might bring, he plunged into the Jabbok, "and a man wrestled with him (there) until the breaking of the day." Who was this nameless deity? A river demon?

Or, perhaps, something more? So Jacob blurted out, "Tell me thy name!"

Is not Jacob and his weird and eerie struggle in the dark with some nameless deity perhaps a reflection of our own times? Maybe this age of anxiety of ours is the crossing of the Jabbok in modern dress and on a world stage. For surely the familiarity of the daily headlines cannot blind us to the weird and eerie quality of life in the mid-twentieth century, as if it were a nightmare, a bad dream, some unknown demon wrestling with us in the dark.

Here, for example, is this strange unpopularity that we Americans have somehow won for ourselves in so many parts of the world. Every other week, it seems, a demonstration or a riot breaks out somewhere in the world and more often than not the target is the American embassy. Surely this must be a bad dream! For obviously all we Americans want is good will and peace and prosperity for everybody, and yet in one country after another we have become in fact "The Ugly American." Is it all the result of communist propaganda and lies? Or is it perhaps, in part at least, our past catching up with us, like Jacob at the Jabbok, a nightmare in the dark.

Or here is the spectre of fear of the darker-skinned races erupting into apartheid in South Africa, or the spectacle of civil rights workers molested or shot down in our own South, or the more polite but equally bitter segregation flourishing in the plushier suburbs of New York, Chicago, or Philadelphia, or, for that matter, in any number of labor unions across the land. And the fear is sharpened by the prospect of a population explosion which will double the number of people on earth from three billion to six billion before our children are as old as some of us are right now. And almost all of those extra three billion will have dark skins. But why are we whites so fearful, we who so solemnly profess our "faith in humanity"? Like any nightmare in the dark, it makes no sense.

Or take the nightmare of our plight in Vietnam where there's little profit in tracing the steps by which we got into the mess we're in. But with few exceptions, most of us are convinced we can't simply pull out and we ought not to be in!

It's a nightmare. A tale told by an idiot. It's a weird and eerie story, the story of these days in which we live, as eerie as a struggle in the dark by the river Jabbok with some nameless deity, when the past catches up with a man or a civilization.

So Jacob, still the shrewd and crafty man of the world, cried, "Tell me thy name!" He still thought he might outwit whatever deity it was that struggled with him there in the dark.

And there's many a shrewd man of the world today, too, caught in the nightmarish struggle of these days, who tries to outwit whatever deity there may be with the cry, "Tell me thy name!" Perhaps the name is "success." So Willie Loman dies by his own hand in *Death of a Salesman,* well liked but a failure, a worthless commodity in a market that goes up or down according to the whims of taste or fashion. Or perhaps the name is "luck." So a man puts his dime in the slot at the railroad station to get his "Lord's Prayer lucky charm." Who knows? If lady Luck works in the daily double, maybe in a world without rhyme or reason—if she should happen to wear a halo—

maybe the lady might work in life too. Or maybe the name is "fate." A friend declares that when he steps on an airliner or steers his car onto a superhighway, he becomes a fatalist. What is to be is to be. Or maybe the name is a faceless deity called "God," the deity imprinted on American stamps and coins, who is obviously favorably disposed to the stars and stripes and unfavorably disposed to those who think we're "ugly." Or maybe the name is a faceless deity, also called God, which we go to meet sometimes in church, where in return for prayers and a dollar bill we'll strike a bargain and get some sleep and peace of mind undisturbed by nightmares. Or maybe the faceless deity is no deity at all, and all we've got on our hands is the grin of the Cheshire cat who has departed long since.

"Tell me your name!" For Jacob in the long night's struggle the cry became a prayer: "I will not let you go unless you bless me." And if our cry too, wrenched out of us by the dark struggle of these times, turns into the prayer, "I will not let you go unless you bless me," we too may receive a blessing. And the blessing? That God will reveal his name, his very nature to us. The name is not success or luck or fate or a faceless deity called God, or even the grin of a Cheshire cat departed long since.

So today in churches scattered all over the world Christians are celebrating the name of God. But it seems to be an uncommonly cumbersome and complicated name for God, the name of the Holy Trinity, Father, Son, and Holy Spirit. And I know perfectly well how impatient people get with this formula which seems so unmanageable and unreal. And I'm holding no brief for any traditional formulation of the doctrine of the Trinity as such. To "accept" a doctrine of the church without struggling with it can be an arid and fruitless business. What is important is that we try to see what kind of struggle in the dark lay behind this cumbersome formula, what kind of living experience led to this queer name for God. For the intent behind it is precisely the answer to the prayer, "Tell me thy name."

What is vital to any understanding or experience of it is to recognize that at the center of the complicated name of the Trinity is the name of Jesus. Start there! For the Holy One, the creative Power, the ultimate Being, that vague, shadowy, and mysterious One whom we call God, had become focused in a life *with* us in history, shedding light and love on those whose lives he touched. The faceless deity has a "face." The great all-seeing Eye is no longer bleak and expressionless, but looks on us in love. Jesus even dared to call this mysterious One "Abba," Father.

Think of it! In the midst of the madness of these days to know that the creator and sustainer of life is one who is with us—Emmanuel—and for us, whose only will for us and for our world is the selfless giving of himself that we have seen in the "Son," in Jesus living and dying on a cross. Whatever nightmares in the dark we have brought upon ourselves are not his doing. If Jesus is at the center of the name of the Trinity, then we can in all boldness and confidence know that God's nature, his very life and being, is love, and that his name is "Father."

But Jesus lived and died long years ago. What about here and now? How can we say that God is with us and for us at this moment?

I was once asked to sit in on a bull session at a top-notch college. It included a fascinating cross section of viewpoints. Some of the students were frankly agnostic. Some were on the fence. Some were troubled but seeking. Some were openly Christian. They were drawn together on that evening by an unspoken desire to probe God's "name" —if there is a God. Without any guidance from anybody they started talking. First they talked about God, the shadowy creator and sustainer of life. But that led inevitably into speculation and a general fog. So someone raised the question, but what about Christ? That gave concreteness to the discussion but still left their crucial question untouched. So one of them finally blurted out, "But what I really want to know is, where can I find God here and now?" And that's what you and I would like to know too, isn't it so? That the Holy One, focused in history in the life and death of Christ, is present with us here and now, available for comfort, enlightenment, guidance, and strength. And that's precisely what the third term in the complicated formula of the Trinity, the Holy Spirit, tries to express. Not a vague, nameless demon wrestling with us in the dark, but the very Holy One himself, his inner being disclosed in the life and death of Christ, present now, offering and demanding love and life that neither death nor hell nor the madness of these days can extinguish.

Those young students had found in their own wrestling with the problem of God the need for the "name" which the church has provided down through the centuries: Father, Son, and Holy Spirit.

And perhaps the fact that many people today experience only the "absence" of God may actually be the work of

God "with" us after all! So Paul Tillich writes: "It is the work of the Spirit that removes God from our sight, not only for some men, but sometimes for many in a particular period. We live in an era in which the God we know is the absent God. But in knowing God as the absent God, we *know* of him; we feel his absence as the empty space which is left by something or someone which belonged to us and has vanished from our view. . . . The spirit has shown to our time and to innumerable people in our time the absent God and the space which cries in us to be filled with him. And then the absent one may return and take the space which belongs to him, and the Spiritual Presence may break again into our consciousness, awakening us to recognize what we are, shaking and transforming us. This may happen like the coming of a storm, the storm of the Spirit, stirring up the stagnant air of our spiritual life."[1]

So perhaps the experience of God "absent" is the work of the Spirit—of God himself—to make us aware of the fact that whether there is a God alive and present here and now or not is serious business. It wasn't serious business for Jacob until that dark night along the Jabbok. Maybe that's the purpose to be found in the nightmare of these days, to shake us out of any complacent acceptance of what we used to mean by the word "God," and make us wrestle with the "name," the clue to his very nature and existence. Not simply so that we can live through these days with a measure of sanity and inward peace, but so that we can come at them courageously and creatively in sure confidence that God's will of love will be done,

[1] Paul Tillich, *The Eternal Now* (New York: Scribner, 1963), p. 88.

not only back there in the distant past of biblical times, but here—now. For the cumbersome name of the Trinity says precisely this: God is not only above and beyond all our imaginings, but he is with us now as once he lived on earth among us, and we can know it if, like Jacob at the Jabbok, we will struggle through the long dark night until the day dawns with the prayer wrung from our lips, "I will not let you go unless you bless me."

PART II

"Blessed is he that is not offended . . ."

The Paradox
in Living Like a Christian

I suspect that a good deal of the confusion regarding the relevance and validity of the Christian faith in our time results from a confusion concerning the image we hold of what a Christian looks like. What *does* a Christian look like? The pictures in our minds run from a negative image, the Christian as a man who avoids what he assumes to be the obvious vices of liquor, gambling, and sex; to the positive but remote image of a man like Dr. Paul E. Carlson, the medical missionary martyred in the Congo; to all way stations in between: the good Joe who goes to church, the insufferable, self-righteous, and prejudiced prig who also goes to church, the man dedicated to social justice who never enters a church—and on and on.

What does a Christian look like—actually? Hence the subject, the paradox in living like a Christian. It may seem strange to call it a paradox. For almost everybody assumes that a Christian is a man who lives by the golden rule, obeys the Ten Commandments, tries to put into daily practice the Sermon on the Mount, and follows his Lord's example of love. And at first glance the New Testament would seem to bear this out. We are told to love

God, do good to our enemies, feed the hungry, clothe the naked, and be a neighbor to the man in need. All we need, apparently, is the will to do it.

The only trouble with that is that the Christian life is also described in the New Testament in such a way that no one could possibly achieve it by an act of the will. Leaf through the pages of the New Testament sometime and see how often the Christian life is described in terms which cannot possibly be achieved by effort or even by obedience. It's far too delicate and fragile a thing to be captured by screwing up our will power to the point of effort or achievement.

At one point, for example, Paul writes, "Rejoice in the Lord alway: and again I say, rejoice" (Phil. 4:4, KJV). And that has always struck me as a little ridiculous. For the one thing you cannot possibly produce on command is joy. Joy is always something given. It's a result, a response, something you cannot possibly achieve by flexing your muscles or turning your brains inside out or following rules. And yet Paul is right, of course. The Christian life at its deepest and highest is always marked by joy.

Moreover, Paul speaks of the Christian life as a "fragrance": "We are the aroma of Christ to God . . . [spreading] the fragrance of the knowledge of him everywhere" (II Cor. 2:14-15). And this is not just a biblical analogy. Carl Sandburg uses the same figure of speech in describing Jesus:

This Jesus was good to look at, smelled good, listened good. He threw out something fresh and beautiful

111

from the skin of his body and the touch of his hands
wherever he passed along.[1]

Like joy, it's obvious that we can't manufacture a Christian "fragrance" either, no matter how hard we try. And
yet a man who has actually caught the spirit or the mind
of Christ does have a certain air about him which you can
sense, and yet you cannot tie it to any particular deeds or
efforts. It is the very lack of effort in a man's concern for
others which gives him this air or "fragrance."

Or to turn to the teachings of Jesus himself, there is
that striking parable of the last judgment made between
the sheep and the goats. And the striking thing about the
sheep is the fact that they were not even aware that they
were doing anything particularly religious or Christian:
"When did we see thee hungry and feed thee, or thirsty
and give thee drink?" (Matt. 25:37-39).

And again it's perfectly clear that a man cannot work
or will to do that which he's not even aware of when he's
done it! This is far beyond any mere obedience to golden
rules or divine commandments; the will has become one
with the will of God. And this *is* living like a Christian:
that the mind of Christ shall have become so a part of us
that our natural, spontaneous impulse is to feed the hungry,
visit the imprisoned, and show hospitality to the outcast.

Arthur Gossip, the great Scottish preacher of a generation ago, uses a suggestive analogy for this same delicate

---

[1] From "To a Contemporary Bunkshooter" from *Chicago Poems* by
Carl Sandburg. Copyright 1916 by Holt, Rinehart and Winston, Inc.
Copyright 1944 by Carl Sandburg. Reprinted by permission of Holt,
Rinehart and Winston, Inc.

and fragile quality of life in an unforgettable sermon, *The Galilean Accent:* "Only when to think in Christ's way has become as instinctive and spontaneous and natural and unconscious as the dialect of one's native place—and whoever notices his own accent, or is so much as aware that it exists?—only when in Paul's phrase we have put on Christ's mind and made it our mind . . . are we fully Christian men and women."[2]

All right. Here is this delicate and fragile quality of the Christian life as it is suggested by joy, fragrance, spontaneous and unself-conscious acts of love, a quality like a man's native accent which betrays where he's naturally at home. How do we get it?

We certainly cannot will to have it. And no matter how many rules you draw up for yourself: do unto others as you would have them do unto you, do a kind deed every day, keep away from smoking, drinking, gambling, and making out, go to church and say your prayers, read your Bible, throw yourself into social problems and into the struggle for civil rights, work for planned parenthood . . . make the list as long as you like and double it in Lent and it won't help! In Jesus' day the Pharisees had worked out over six hundred thou shalts and thou shalt nots and they willed to obey them and they did! Let's not underestimate the will power and diligent effort and obedience that marked the lives of the most religious men of his day. And yet they did not capture that elusive joy or fragrance or unself-conscious giving of themselves to the needs of the neighbor. In fact, it turned out just the opposite. Some

2 Arthur J. Gossip, *The Galilean Accent* (Edinburgh: T. & T. Clark, 1926), p. 3.

of them did have a fragrance about them, all right, but
it was the fragrance of dead men's bones and all unclean-
ness. And that still happens when people think that living
like a Christian is made up solely of rules and effort and
will power, of sheer obedience. No wonder people with
sensitive noses steer clear of some church people!

Here, then, is the paradox in living like a Christian. It's
obvious we can't just sit on our hands and wait for the
Spirit of God to move us to acts of love; and yet if we
spit on our hands and go to work, apparently that's not
going to get us anywhere either so far as capturing the essential quality of the Christian life is concerned.

How then, can we resolve the paradox? Well, strangely
enough, you do work in the hope of achieving it, but you
don't work at the thing itself. Perhaps a couple of ana-
logies will help.

One weekend one of my daughters and a friend of hers
were home from college and they were talking about the
problem some girls had in getting dates—and they were
attractive girls, too. The problem, they said, was that these
girls were so anxious to fall in love and get married that
they looked at each date as a potential husband, worked
so hard and got so tense about the whole business that the
boys were scared off. It's an old story, of course. A girl
who works night and day at falling in love will probably
miss the real thing. And yet, on the other hand, it's obvious a girl does have to work at it. She can't just sit
home twiddling her thumbs and hope! She has to work
at it in the sense of making herself available and attractive and meeting boys. And if she does work at it in this
sense, then some day it may happen, this mysterious at-

traction between a man and a woman that results in love and marriage. But if she works at the thing itself, chances are, she'll miss it.

Or to take another area of experience, here is a writer and this mysterious thing called "inspiration" which can lift mediocre writing to the level of good writing and, occasionally, to the level of great or "inspired" writing. Top-notch writers invariably say that this "inspiration" does not come unless they give themselves to the discipline and drudgery of regular hours of work each day. They sit down and write whether the spirit is on them or not. If they do, then sometimes it comes. But if they work at getting the thing itself, great writing, they get tied in knots and miss it altogether.

So, then, with the Christian life. We cannot possibly achieve the delicate and fragile quality of life which marks living like a Christian at its deepest and highest by working at it, but we nevertheless work. You discipline yourself. You act out of duty and obedience. How often Paul, who describes the Christian life as a "fragrance," nevertheless tells us to work at it: "Be imitators of God. . . . Practice hospitality. . . . Pray without ceasing." All this takes conscious effort even though all this effort will not give you the mind of Christ. Strange, isn't it? The one thing we cannot possibly capture by direct assault, simply by effort, can come to us only as we give ourselves to the effort.

But embedded in the effort must be some kind of desire on our part to have this strange, elusive quality of life. Jesus put it this way: "Blessed are those who hunger and thirst for righteousness, for they shall be satisfied" (Matt.

5:6). But this desire, too, we cannot achieve by trying, by blowing on our hands and putting our backs into it. If you happen to like music, whether Bach, Beethoven, Joan Baez, or the Beatles, you did not come by it by trying. You were exposed to it, possibly captivated by it, until a love, a desire for it, developed. So with the good life.

What is it about Christ that attracts you? That draws you to him in curiosity or in wonder? Perhaps it's his gentleness with the outcasts and unlovely that draws you at first. Or, perhaps, it's his courage in the face of opposition, betrayal, and death. Or perhaps it's his impatience with rules and regulations and the inner integrity of his spirit. Or perhaps it's the disturbing, probing presence of love broken on a cross, the haunting notion that here is the clue to ultimate reality, to what's at the center of this baffling existence of ours to give it purpose and meaning. Joachim Probst, the painter, who has never been inside the door of a church, has yet painted the crucifixion over and over again in violent, even brutal, color and form. He is reported to have said, "I don't know what it means. But if there is meaning anywhere, I suspect it is there." Whatever it is that awakens a desire in you to draw near, to know more about him, this is how the delicate quality of the Christian life takes root and grows in a man, naturally and spontaneously.

There's only one qualification to this desire. Helmut Thielicke has pointed out[8] that God is not at all interested in what we are most willing to surrender to him—time, money, even a career. God insists on entering our lives

---

[8] Helmut Thielicke, *The Waiting Father* (New York: Harper and Row, 1959), p. 188.

precisely at the point where we put up the biggest resistance: maybe it's sex, or ambition, or intellectual pride, or insistence on my rights. Whatever it is, *there* is where God obstinately insists on entering my life, your life. The desire, therefore, must be focused precisely at the point where we want him least!

And if that is to happen, then obviously the desire needs to be constantly nourished and strengthened. And for that I can think of nothing but this: To live much each day with Christ. I know exactly how pious that sounds, how much like a sermon. And yet I can find no clearer phrase. If we say, to live much each day with God, the trouble is that "God" can be interpreted in too many different ways and goodness can be made to fit any kind of conduct which appeals to us at the moment. Hitler, you remember, appealed to his own picture of God to slaughter six million Jews. Even "Christ" is not foolproof, of course. There are those who use the word to justify segregation and to raise free enterprise to the level of a Christian absolute. But if we say, "To live much each day with Christ," it ought to be clear that to live with God is to live with a very specific, definite quality of life before our eyes.

For we tend to become like that with which we live and spend much of our time. A man who spends much of his time in burlesque houses and looking at suggestive pictures and reading salacious books and magazines will grow in his preoccupation with sex as lust until there comes a time when he can no longer free his imagination from it by his own will without outside help. Or a woman whose waking hours are filled with thoughts of her own ailments, real though they may be, whose conversation constantly turns in on herself, her doctors and nostrums, diets and operations, will soon be suffering from imaginary ailments from which she will not be able to free herself by her own will without outside help.

More positively, this is why students of art, science, music, or literature will want to work under some master in the field, not merely to learn techniques and methods, but to catch some "plus," something of the spirit of the man so that they, with their own individuality and peculiar gifts may express something of that same creative spirit in their own work. We tend to become like that with which we live and spend much of our time.

What are the things which fill your thoughts and imaginations, hour by hour, day by day? Are they selfish, shallow, petty? Then you are becoming like that. Inexorably. Or are your thoughts on better things? Listen to Paul: "Brethren, whatsoever things are true, whatsoever things are honest . . . whatsoever things are of good report; if there be any virtue . . . think on these things" (Phil. 4:8, KJV). Not in abstractions or as disembodied qualities of the good life, but as you see these things concretely in the flesh and blood figure of Christ.

You cannot make yourself good by trying. But this you can do. You can bring into your mind and flood your imagination with the picture of incarnate love as he moves about offering friendship to the outcasts and unlovable or calling for single-minded devotion; dealing gently with the perplexed and the doubting or blasting away at the proud and self-righteous; humbly washing the feet of his disciples or offering himself as a sacrifice for a world that rejects him. And if you live with him much each day, you will tend to be changed little by little into his likeness— if this is what you really want above everything else! So Paul: "And we all, with unveiled face, beholding the glory of the Lord, are being changed into his likeness from one degree of glory to another; for this comes from the Lord who is the Spirit" (II Cor. 3:18).

And then—if it comes—you won't even be aware of it. It will be as natural as a native accent, as unconscious as the acts of love and concern of the sheep in the parable. Indeed, you may have something of it even now. But don't go looking for it! For if you recognize it in yourself, it's not the real thing. The best thing about it is that you don't know whether you have it or not, the mind of Christ, the fragrance, the accent of the true Christian which betrays the place where he's naturally at home.

This is why the Christian life is a life lived in trust, in faith, rather than a life lived solely by rules and principles and commandments. For you and I know perfectly well that anything we achieve by our own will and effort always comes far short of the mind of Christ, far short of what God requires of us; and we are never sure whether we have fulfilled his will of love in anything we have ever done. But we live our lives in daily obedience, doing what we believe ought to be done—failing all along the line—but not worrying ourselves sick about it, *trusting* that he who works so mysteriously through the puny efforts of the likes of you and me will forgive the failures and, perhaps, give even to us something of the aroma, the fragrance, the unconscious accent of a man who is at home with the God we have seen in the face of Christ.

A Bad Bargain

"For the kingdom of heaven is like a householder who went out early in the morning to hire laborers for his vineyard. After agreeing with the laborers for a denarius a day, he sent them into his vineyard. And going out about the third hour he saw others standing idle in the market place; and to them he said, 'You go into the vineyard too, and whatever is right I will give you.' So they went. Going out again about the sixth hour and the ninth hour, he did the same. And about the eleventh hour he went out and found others standing; and he said to them, 'Why do you stand here idle all day?' They said to him, 'Because no one has hired us.' He said to them, 'You go into the vineyard too.' And when evening came, the owner of the vineyard said to his steward, 'Call the laborers and pay them their wages, beginning with the last, up to the first.' And when those hired about the eleventh hour came, each of them received a denarius. Now when the first came, they thought they would receive more; but each of them also received a denarius. And on receiving it they grumbled at the householder, saying, 'These last worked only one hour, and you have made them equal to us who have borne the burden of the day and the scorching heat.' But he replied to one of them, 'Friend, I am doing you no wrong; did you not agree with me for a denarius? Take what belongs to you, and go; I choose to give to this last as I give to you. Am I not allowed to do what I choose with what belongs to me? Or do you begrudge my generosity?' So the last will be first, and the first last." —*Matthew 20:1-16*

Our point of reference at the moment is one of the parables of Jesus, this strange story of the way an employer handled his employees and their predictable reactions.

I'm not sure what you may think of the parables of Jesus, if anything, but they're not cozy little folk tales with an obvious moral attached, nor are they complicated allegories, each detail hiding some esoteric meaning known only to the initiated. Rather are they readings from life, like any good novel, but with this difference: Each one views life from the perspective of the freedom and love of God, which is why it begins, "The kingdom of heaven is like . . . ."

In other words, here is a slice of life served up as Jesus sees it. Whether it is also true to your own experience or not is for you to decide.

No doubt our first reaction to the story is that it's certainly a crazy, mixed-up way of running the world if this householder in the parable of the laborers and the hours is supposed to provide a clue. Five times during the day he goes out to get laborers for his vineyard and then at the end of the day pays them all the same wage. No wonder the ones hired first were burned up. They *had* been burned by the heat of the sun all day long while the ones hired last, when the sun was low, played it cool in more ways than one and got just as much pay as the first.

What sense does it make? What happens to our tidy world of balance sheets, profit and loss, and an "honest day's work for an honest day's wage"? What has happened to just plain ordinary justice here? And what has happened to other passages in the New Testament which suggest that it is eternally significant what a man does with his life where judgment is based on what is actually *done* through the long heat of the day to "the least of these, my brethren." But on the basis of this story, you might as well eat, drink, and be merry, or lounge around in bed all your life if you'd rather, or get after it with all the wits and training you can get, make your name and perhaps even a fortune, and then "come to Jesus" at the end and everything will turn out all right.

Some learned scholars have suggested that it's a picture of God's pity on the dispossessed. He gives in response to need rather than on the basis of work accomplished, a kind of heavenly welfare state where through God's mercy everyone gets taken care of regardless of his labor. Well, I might just buy that as a woolly-headed liberal, overlooking the injustice of it, were it not for the fact that this is no picture of God's boundless generosity, "good measure, pressed down, shaken together, and running over." A denarius, the daily wage given, was a pittance actually, just about enough to keep body and soul together for twenty-four hours. It was worth about twenty cents. And even in those days that was no fortune.

So what's the point? Fortunately, some of the parables of Jesus were placed in a context which provides a clue to their meaning. This is one of them. Matthew places it in a series of events which leads up to it.

If you back up a bit into the nineteenth chapter, you find the familiar story of the rich young man who "turned away sorrowfully" when Jesus pointed out that his wealth would have to go if he were to have "treasure in heaven." The lesson is clear. It's not that wealth is a bad thing, necessarily, nor that everyone is expected to become a

pauper to get in good with God. Rather is it God's insistence on having every part of us and particularly that
which we are least willing to give up. This makes sense.
If God is God—if there is a God—obviously he's not interested in 50 per cent of us or 75 per cent of us or even
95 per cent of us; it's all or nothing. For the rich man
that which he hung on to for dear life was his money,
and that may still be true for some of us. For someone
else it might be intellectual pride or prejudice or ambition
or a secure slot in the scheme of things for his kids. Whatever it is that we want most to hold back, that is precisely
what God has his eye on.

Now Peter and the disciples were watching all this. And
they got the point; it was all too clear. And inevitably
they applied it to themselves. After all, they *had* given
up everything, "goods, fame, child, and wife." So Peter:
"Lo, we have left all and followed you. What then shall
we have?" It was a natural question. Peter thought he
had stumbled on the ultimate secret to human life and
destiny and he couldn't resist getting it down in black and
white. Like the boy watching a cat pounce on an unsus-
pecting sparrow and muttering to himself, "Ah! So that's
it!" So Peter, watching the young man turn away and
then putting reverse english on the incident: "So that's
how life operates! Lo, we have left all and followed you.
What then shall we have?"

The answer Jesus gave did not disappoint Peter though
it might surprise us. For the answer did in fact support
Peter's hunch. Jesus was completely reassuring. Peter was
dead right, apparently. "Truly I say to you . . . when the
Son of Man shall sit on his glorious throne, you who have

followed me will also sit on thrones, judging the twelve tribes of Israel. And every one who has left houses or brothers or sisters or father or mother or children or lands for my sake, will receive a hundredfold and inherit eternal life." Well, there it was! Not a bad bargain at all! Sacrifices here, to be sure, and not cheap or easy ones either—no cheap grace!—but rewards to dazzle you forever afterward.

If that were all there were to it, it would make great sense. This kind of operation is understandable. To be sure, like the rich young ruler, we might not be willing to make the sacrifice. And I don't suppose the image of sitting on thrones moves you particularly or that the phrase "eternal life," bare and unadorned, strikes much of a fire in your hearts. But at least a man knows where he stands. *Quid pro quo.* Meet the terms set and the reward—if you happen to want it—follows. Here we are quite at home. Pass the road test and get your driver's license. Meet the demands of term papers and examinations and get the grade and eventually the diploma. Do your research, publish, and get tenure. Save your money, live within your budget, and get financial security. This is ordinary justice and familiar ground. Of course we may try to beat the system; there must be an angle somewhere! But this is the way run-of-the-mill Americans have always gotten ahead in life. And if this is the way God operates, even though his demands may be severe, at least it makes sense. It may be a hard bargain, but it's a bargain. All you do with respect to God, his demand and his reward, is raise it all to the nth degree.

But. . . . There's always God's "but." And after the

"but" comes this perplexing parable of the laborers in the vineyard which throws the whole neat scheme of things into a shambles. The *quid pro quo* falls apart. The understandable equation of sacrifice-reward falls to the ground. No wonder the first group of workers were upset. They had entered into a contract, all neat and tidy, an agreement for a day's wage for a day's work. But . . . "These last worked only one hour, and you have made them equal to us who have borne the burden of the day and the scorching heat." Notice, please, that the promised reward *is still there!* But suddenly it has turned sour and rancid. The bargain with God turns from a hard bargain into a bad bargain. Why is this so?

Well, first of all we are reminded here that reward *is* part and parcel of the biblical record. Some serious-minded but squeamish theological students I've known through the years have been embarrassed by this continual biblical emphasis upon reward: eternal life, abundant life, treasure in heaven, sitting on thrones, pie in the sky. God, they feel, ought not to offer rewards. It's beneath his dignity and ours. Maybe it would be better to call us to an absurd kind of courage which might well lead to nothingness! At least they'd be far happier if all these gaudy promises were cut out of the biblical record entirely.

But the presence of reward in the Bible simply means that life has its inevitable results. Life is not meaningless. Events have their consequences. Life moves to its inevitable decision in the presence of God. There is judgment. You reap what you sow. Not tasty but unfortunately true. And the other side of judgment is reward. We are utterly dependent upon God now and in the future. Our times are in his hands. The unfaithful will have their reward and so will the faithful.

The picture gets distorted as soon as we look at the promised reward in terms of purpose, as soon as we look at it with Peter's calculating eye: "What then shall we have?" As one New Testament scholar puts it, "Jesus' attitude is indeed paradoxical; he promises reward to those who are obedient without thought of reward." Nowhere is this paradoxical attitude painted in more vivid colors than in the parable of the last judgment with the division made between the sheep and the goats. And who are the sheep? They are those naïve souls who were not even aware they were doing anything particularly religious or even Christian; certainly there was no thought of a reward dangling before their noses. They are utterly taken aback at their reward: "When saw we thee hungry and fed thee? . . . When saw we thee naked?" It was this uncalculating response to the man in need which brought the "reward." The goats worked on precisely the opposite principle, which is why they were goats.

But is this, after all, so foreign to our own experience? Even in our tit for tat normal way of living, there come occasional moments when we act without thought of return, like sparks thrown off from the wheels of a train going its ordered way along the tracks. There's the impulse to join the Peace Corps, for example. No doubt the motives are mixed. But sometimes it's not simply to get out of a rut or away from the affluent society or to broaden one's experience; sometimes it's simply to see what it's like to devote your life for a time to nothing but serving others who need what you have to give. Or, at a more ordinary level, there's the impulse to do what you can for the bereaved family next door without looking for anything in return. All Jesus is saying is that these occasional outbursts of sympathy and concern without calculation of getting something back in kind, are the norm in God's world. Everything else in our tit for tat world is abnormal.

I grant you such a quixotic way of life would make a shambles of the business world or the world of politics or international affairs where life, for all its complexity, is actually far simpler, far more orderly and predictable. There we operate with an eye on the calculated effect: So much foreign aid equals so much good will for the good old USA; so much investment equals so much return; a sizable contribution to a political party equals so much consideration for the problems of General Motors or the AFL-CIO; do a favor now, for who knows when we may need a favor in return! No doubt we have to operate that way, being the calculating creatures that we are. But in our relationship to God and to the human beings around us, this other quixotic arrangement of uncalculating love is the only possible arrangement.

For notice how the contractual arrangement with the householder in the parable distorted the relationship of the first laborers to those hired later. If the first ones hired had been the only ones in the picture, there would have been no problem! But as soon as these others came into the picture, a deadly comparison entered too, and with it came animosity, jealousy, and the desire for "justice." You see the same thing happening in the story of the prodigal son. The elder brother worked under a kind of contractual arrangement with the father. He stayed home, minded his *p*'s and *q*'s, saved his money, went to church regularly, and so—he figured—got his father's love and respect in return. But when his father threw a party for the prodigal brother after he had left home, sowed his wild oats, squandered his money, and ended in a pigsty instead of a church, the relationship with the younger brother was poisoned. It never fails. Get your tit for tat arrangement into your relationship with God, and our relationship with our neighbors is poisoned at the spring.

This is why the popular notion that "what I believe is my own business," this notion that religion is completely an individual affair, is so contrary to the way the Bible reads life. What you believe about God invariably colors your relationship to other people. If your business with God is on a business-like basis, so much faithfulness and obedience equals so much reward either here or hereafter, then the neighbor becomes a competitor, an enemy really, who has to be forced into the same tit for tat pattern. I will resent or at least envy (secretly, of course) another's happiness or good fortune. "Why should he? . . . When I . . .?" So I will resent the Negro driving around in a Cadillac when I have to be content with a Chevrolet—or a Cadillac, for that matter! For obviously I deserve the Cadillac. So a bargain with God on whatever terms is a bad bargain because it distorts and poisons my relationship to others around me.

But it's also a bad bargain because it distorts my relationship to God too. Because it inevitably leads me to think that I have God under some modicum of my control, at least. For if God doesn't live up to my understanding of his end of the bargain, I can throw tantrums or, more probably, "lose my faith," as we say, which is simply a way of trying to get God under my control. Poor old God, you know, I don't believe in him any more! And that is putting the cart before the horse, isn't it so? The grumbling of the first workers was not simply a matter of injustice or a distortion of their relationship to the other workers; in effect it was their reluctance to let God be God. So the householder replies to their griping, "Am I not allowed to do what I choose with what is mine? Do you begrudge my generosity?"

And that *would* be a crazy way to run a world, to cut God down to the size of our *quid pro quo,* to our sense of justice. For even at best, our notions of justice are partial and inperfect. Even in our courts of law, rarely do we attempt to probe the motives behind the act, in grand larceny for example. And even if we do, as in the attempt to pinpoint "malice aforethought" in a homicide, the results are at best tentative. For who can probe the mixture of motives which underline our outward acts? And we, therefore, should tell God how to act? Prescribe for him what is just and unjust?

Better, I suspect, to follow Christ's lead here as this parable is told in the context of the rich young man who turned away, Peter's calculating question, and the promise of thrones offered to the faithful. The remarkable thing about it is that our Lord loved the rich young man who turned away, just as he loved Peter who sacrificed everything but wanted to tally up what was in it for him, just as God loves us with our alternating moods of faith too little and too late, of sacrifice, of calculating self-interest. And it's that kind of love we are asked to trust here.

It all adds up to the fact that in God's strange economy, you can't count on anything except him. Draw up your rules by which life ought to be governed, a nicely calculated tit for tat, plan your strategy for coming to terms with it all, plot your "M. O.," structure it in terms of common-sense justice, make it as neat and tidy as you can, and God immediately steps outside of it all laughing—not derisively!—but with a kind of holy hilarity! "Trust me with your obedience and don't count the cost"—which is familiar enough—"but don't count on the results either or the whole thing will turn sour and rancid. Make a bargain with me and it will turn into a bad bargain. But trust me with your life and love and. . . . Well, if you've got your eye on what follows the 'and,' you've got your eyes on the wrong place to begin with. Listen: 'The kingdom of heaven is like a householder who went out early in the morning to hire laborers for his vineyard . . . .' "

God's Incredible Optimism

And when a great crowd came together and people from town after town came to him, he said in a parable: "A sower went out to sow his seed; and as he sowed, some fell along the path, and was trodden under foot, and the birds of the air devoured it. And some fell on the rock; and as it grew up, it withered away, because it had no moisture. And some fell among thorns; and the thorns grew with it and choked it. And some fell into good soil and grew, and yielded a hundredfold." As he said this, he called out, "He who has ears to hear, let him hear."　　　　—*Luke 8:4-8*

"For as the rain and the snow come down from heaven,
　and return not thither but water the earth,
making it bring forth and sprout,
　giving seed to the sower and bread to the eater,
so shall my word be that goes forth from my mouth;
　it shall not return to me empty,
but it shall accomplish that which I purpose,
　and prosper in the thing for which I sent it."
　　　　—*Isaiah 55:10-11*

The parable of the sower is a preacher's piece of cake because it offers so many delightful possibilities in the interpretation of it. For one thing it suggests the percentages involved, for the odds are obviously against Christ and his church: only one out of the four soils proves productive. But for the gambler there's still that one man in four!

Or, perhaps, we take the parable as a bit of Jesus' auto-biography. He had a tough time of it too, preaching, teaching, healing, and with such meagre results. And so we end up feeling sorry for poor old Jesus and for ourselves. It's a grim, rough road but we can garner a little satisfaction in the hope that perhaps we may be among those in the tiny minority that produced results.

Or—as we preachers usually do—we can turn to the three unproductive soils and mess around in them for twenty minutes or so, relishing the opportunity to vent our frustrations on those three characters we know so well because the church seems to be so full of them: the beaten path—the tough customer who never has responded and never will. Or the thin soil covering rock—the shallow enthusiast who gushes all over the place at every new venture, but ten minutes later, when you hit the long pull, he's faded away. Or the ground filled with weeds and thorns—the hot prospect whose only trouble is that he's a hot prospect for everything that comes down the pike, whether for cares and anxieties or riches and pleasures of this life, and so everything takes root and grows in his life; it's a jungle.

And although there may be a bit of truth in each of these possible interpretations, the parable lends itself properly to but two basic approaches. One is pessimistic. Helmut Thielicke, one of the great preacher-theologians of our time, opens a sermon by saying, "I wonder if we have caught the sadness that hangs over this story. . . . There is in this parable a deep sense of grief and sorrow."[1]

[1] Helmut Thielicke, *The Waiting Father* (New York: Harper and Row, 1959), p. 52.

On the other hand, A. M. Hunter, a contemporary New Testament scholar, finds great optimism here: "The parable carries a ringing assurance for faint-hearted disciples. . . . In spite of all frustrations and failures, God's Rule advances, and his harvest exceeds all expectations. Courage! Have faith in God."[2]

Well, which is right? Probably both are true, but the optimism overcomes the pessimism. The pointed thrust of the parable comes at the end. The odds may be only one in four but the harvest in that *one,* the good soil, is something to behold! In this connection it is interesting to compare the three versions of the parable. Matthew's account is the most cautious. He starts off boldly enough, "And some fell into good soil and yielded a hundredfold." But then like any good theologian, he thinks twice and ends more cautiously, "some sixty and some thirty." Mark reverses it all and builds up to the big, optimistic climax: "some thirty, some sixty, some a hundredfold." Luke is forthright: "A hundredfold." And that's a veritable bumper crop since even a tenfold harvest was considered par for the course and ten times ten is quite a recovery on the investment. Though the pessimism is in the story, of course, and we'll get to that in a moment, the overarching thrust of the parable is incredibly optimistic in the deepest sense of the word. And so we'll start there, even at the risk of an anticlimax later on. The parable is an unforgettable story of God's incredible optimism.

But note in the first place that the optimism is not a simple reflection of good times for the church and Christ's

[2] A. M. Hunter, *Interpreting the Parables* (Naperville, Ill.: SCM Book Club, 1960), p. 47.

kingdom. The situation out of which it came does not determine its dominant mood like so many of our interpretations of it. When Helmut Thielicke finds a "sadness hanging over the story," it's understandable. His sermon was first delivered during the resistance movement in Germany when Hitler and the Nazi regime were in full sway. Small wonder he sees primarily the unproductive soils. In contrast we might say that the optimistic interpretation is simply the product of fifteen years or so of relative peace and prosperity after the end of the war. But this theory doesn't square with the facts. The parable apparently was first uttered by Jesus midstream in his career. The first flush of success, the enthusiastic crowds which greeted him wherever he went, had paled. Now there was growing opposition, misunderstanding, fair weather disciples. As Jeremias, the noted New Testament scholar, suggests,[3] the occasion was an atmosphere permeated by doubts, so similar to our situation today, doubts occasioned by the apparently ineffectual preaching of Jesus, bitter hostility and increasing defections from the ranks of his followers, all of which seemed to contradict the claims of Christ's mission. The undergirding optimism was not simply a reflection of what we might call a successful ministry.

Moreover, consider the parallel passage in the Old Testament at the end of the fifty-fifth chapter of Isaiah, where the unknown prophet of the Exile speaks in God's behalf: "So shall my word be that goes forth from my mouth; it shall not return to me empty, but it shall accomplish that which I purpose, and prosper in the thing for which I sent

[3] Joachim Jeremias, *The Parables of Jesus* (New York: Scribner, 1963), p. 151.

it." This tremendous outpouring of divine optimism with respect to God's purpose for the world came out of an all but hopeless situation, at the end of fifty long years in exile, when almost everyone had given up hope of deliverance or of the power of God to do anything about the situation. If God was not dead, he was impotent.

Maybe it takes a tough situation before we can really grasp the tremendous optimism of God. When things are going well, the optimism gets thin. Before our time of troubles, beginning roughly fifty years ago, there were a lot of optimistic Christians around. But it was pretty thin stuff. They talked of man's inherent goodness, of the evangelization of the world in one generation, of automatic progress which they borrowed from Darwin and promptly applied to the Bible and to the Christian movement ever since. You and I know better! The inherent goodness in man ran afoul of Auschwitz and Buchenwald; the evangelization of the world in one generation ran up against communism and nihilism abroad and against the beat generation and culture religion at home; and automatic progress went down the drain in the all-but-forgotten misery of a world-wide depression, the fall of colonial empires and the mushroom clouds over Hiroshima and Nagasaki. We may be sitting just a trifle more comfortably these days but we're not apt to embrace any easygoing optimism either. Not with the mess in Vietnam and the unsolved problems of race, poverty, and the population explosion.

And certainly not with respect to the Christian enterprise! To be sure, our churches are still pretty full and the coffers are still well lined, and we like to protest that this is still a Christian nation "under God." But you and I know that the church has been in retreat for some time. With a few exceptions, it has pulled up its skirts and run from the inner city. It was just about the last institution to get on the bandwagon for civil rights when it should have been leading the parade. Billy Graham is reported to have said that he suspected that in some areas the church would be the last institution to give in to integration. Moreover, the Christian faith really cuts very little ice where the decisions that count in our world are made: in the board rooms of banks and corporations, in the legislatures and city councils, in the high councils of the labor unions. And even in the daily decisions made by ordinary people every day, in hiring and firing, buying and selling, taking a job or turning it down, in voting booths or in the private chambers of the safe deposit vaults at the local bank, how often, do you think, does Christian commitment seriously affect these daily decisions? And when you come to the churches and their run-of-the-mill activities, though there are shining exceptions, it's pretty difficult to draw any sharp distinction between the program of the typical Ladies' Aid Society and the local garden club; they're both concerned with interesting hobbies except that the garden club is apt to be far more intriguing. Or listen in on the meeting of a vestry or church board and compare it with the business carried on by the board of directors of the country club. They're both concerned with budgets, buildings and grounds, and the complaints of truculent members.

Really now! Is there much cause for optimism regarding the cause of Christ and his church today? Practically all of the current literature on the renewal of the church makes for dreary reading so far as the church-life we have become accustomed to is concerned. But it's precisely at such a time that we may be open to the thrust of this parable: the incurable and incredible optimism of God! Despite the obvious failures of the church—traced in large part to the ineffectiveness and failures of the likes of you and me—God sows his seed in hope. No! Hope is too mild a word; in divine confidence and assurance that his will *will* be done; his purposes will be achieved.

Frankly, I find it terribly hard to understand and even harder to believe. Maybe in part because I live and work in a community of theological students and faculty who take their Christianity with deadly seriousness. And the seriousness *is* deadly at times: the furrowed brow, the worried look, the rehearsal of our failures and lack of commitment. But if we take this parable seriously, and that means taking the whole Bible seriously, God has no furrowed brow. He's not worried! No doubt he is far from pleased with us and others like us. There's longing in his heart, and concern, and the low grumble of his wrath. And—we can never forget— there's pain in the heart of God; the cross marks the permanent scar which is more than a scar—it's an open wound! But he's not worried! "My word will not return unto me empty!"

Perhaps this accounts for the divine carelessness with which he sows his seed, scattering it into the most unlikely places, into the hearts of all sorts and kinds with a kind of gay abandon: "And some fell by the wayside, and some on the rock, and some among thorns." It's so difficult for us to comprehend. We take our stewardship of time and talents and money so much more seriously! Pulling our

churches out of changing neighborhoods because the results are discouraging and the future looks bleak; making
careful, fact-finding surveys before opening up a new congregation lest we waste the church's money; trying out
various okay methods for renewal of the church and then
if no visible response is evident, shaking the dust of their
unconcern from off our feet; limiting the attention we
give to some people because the prospects don't look very
favorable for response—after all our time is a trust from
God and we must use it where it will do the most good!
I suppose we have to. For what could we report to the
next convention of the church if we have no statistical
results to show for all our labor and money? But isn't it
dreary? This cautious, calculating eye always looking for
measurable results?

For how can you measure the results of God's work in
the world? Or in a man's heart? We've got hard-nosed
sociologists at work all over the place these days measuring the results of the Christian enterprise in the difference
it makes in community structures, in decision making, in
changing the face of the community where it exists. The
findings, as you can guess, are not encouraging. And we
need these sociologists and their probings lest we go on
thinking that a sermon preached and listened to on civil
rights or the evil of narcotics or the breaking up of the
family discharges our responsibility in those areas until the
next sermon comes along. We're always in danger of falling for pious pap and salving our consciences, when the
proof of the pudding is in the eating: "Why do you call
me, Lord, Lord, and do not the things that I say?"

And yet how do you measure the deep places in a man's

heart? The motives? One preacher confessed to preaching a poor sermon but pointed to the power of the Word in it nevertheless because one man who heard it entered the Christian ministry. But how do we know that was for the best? How do we know he might not have made a better Christian as a lawyer or a salesman or a plumber? We have a habit of looking for visible, tangible results and plastering labels on them: good . . . bad. If a man enters the ministry, it must be God's Spirit at work in him; it must be "good." Well, I don't know. I've been getting around to a lot of church dedications in recent years and invariably thanks are offered because God has "blessed" them with a new building. But how do we know it's a blessing—from God? I was pastor of a church some years ago and we built a lovely new building. And I was never sure it was God's will, tangible evidence of his blessing! At the time, there were hundreds of bombed out churches in England and Germany. How do we know the money should not have been spent to rebuild one of *those* churches? Or used in some other way?

I'm skeptical of trying to estimate visible results in churches or in individual lives. I'm all for sociological surveys. We should read, note, and ponder the Peter Bergers, Gibson Winters, Gerhard Lenskis and their incisive diagnoses of a sick church. But my faith does not rest on their findings—good or bad! Which is why I'm skeptical of trying to estimate visible results in churches or in individual lives. And so, apparently, was our Lord— or he would not have bothered! Take his disciples—every one of them presumably an answer to prayer. Peter denied him. James and John argued as to who was to be top dog in the kingdom. Judas betrayed him. And in the end they all forsook him and fled. Those were the tangible, visible results of the sower and his seed when it was scattered on what apparently was the finest soil he could find! After all, he prayed before choosing each of the disciples. Have you ever thought of Judas as an answer to prayer?

If God were tied to our calculating eye fastened on visible and tangible results appearing when and where we want them to appear, there'd be no prophets, no Christ, no church, no Bible. Or to bring it closer to home, there'd be no offer of his love and forgiveness in your direction or mine. For this is what it all adds up to in the end, the embarrassing fact that God is utterly and completely optimistic with respect to the response he expects to find in you. And in me. I suspect if God were not so divinely careless with his Word, more calculating and hardheaded, he'd simply pass us by. But the point of the good soil is that in each one there is the potential to respond. And that potential is not off there somewhere, in somebody else who's more religious perhaps, or more devout, or more obviously committed, or who reads the Bible more frequently, but in you. I know. It's embarrassing. But God is confident that you and I can respond and bear fruit a hundredfold, believe it or not!

Which is why the parable of God's incredible optimism ends, "He who has ears to hear, let him hear." Because we're not spectators to the story, we're in it. God is addressing you. And all those unproductive soils are part of our make-up too, of course, and that's the "sadness that hangs over the story." There's a beaten path in each one of us, a stubborn resistance hardened by years of the traffic of ordinary days, the refusal to give in to love and mercy and justice, and above all to accept the forgiveness offered to us which will break up the hardened crust in our lives and make of us new men. And there's shallow ground in all of us, too, the superficial enthusiasm of the moment which burns out as soon as we face discipline, duty, and patience, particularly in the face of a lack of visible results. And there's thorny ground in every one of us —perhaps more of this than any other—the cares and anxieties which lead us to question, to fail to trust when suffering comes or idiotic tragedy, and the offer of God's love for us is simply choked to death in bitterness or self-pity; or at the opposite pole, the riches and pleasures of this life when things go so supremely well that we scarcely feel the need for God, his care, his forgiveness—with the same result: the divine Word is choked to death.

But there is also good soil in us. There's the need, the desire and ability to respond, the yearning for the deep peace of God in the midst of cares and anxieties, the riches and pleasures. That's there too. And God, incredible optimist that he is, is confident that you will respond. He dreams such great dreams for you and me, "bearing fruit a hundredfold"! But he's not dreaming. God is no worrier. And he's no dreamer. "He who has ears to hear, let him hear." There will be those who hear and respond. It could be you. It could be me. I suspect we'd better get with it. Isn't it so?

The Patience
and Impatience of God

Wait on the Lord: be of good courage, and he shall strengthen thine heart: wait, I say, on the Lord.
—*Psalm 27:14* (KJV)

I wait for the Lord, my soul doth wait, and in his word do I hope.
My soul waiteth for the Lord more than they that watch for the morning; I say, more than they that watch for the morning.   —*Psalm 130:5-6* (KJV)

And that, knowing the time, that now it is high time to awake out of sleep: for now is our salvation nearer than when we believed.
The night is far spent, the day is at hand . . . .
—*Romans 13:11-12a* (KJV)

See then that ye walk circumspectly, not as fools, but as wise, redeeming the time . . . .   —*Ephesians 5:15-16a* (KJV)

A sign at a sharp bend in the road reads, "Lose a minute, save a life." Behind the caution to the motorist driving too fast is a sharp reading of our age. The reason the motorist is driving too fast is precisely to "save a minute." He's in a hurry to get where he's going. Why? To design more time-saving gadgets and faster jet planes to save another minute to get somewhere else in a hurry? Why? To save a life? His own perhaps? To flee the spectre of a mushroom cloud in the sky? Or, more likely, to avoid the blank terror of being alone with himself? It's enough to make you slow down for a minute not only to avoid crashing into a ditch at the sharp bend in the road or to avoid a fifteen dollar fine before the local judge, but to ask, What's your hurry? Why the rush?

"Lose a minute, save a life," and then the sign adds, "For the life you save may be your own." And that comes pretty close to the meaning behind one of the most familiar and most maddening words in the Bible: "Wait! Wait on the Lord. . . . Wait patiently for him." For an age in a rush, smashing speed records and sound barriers; for an age whose most characteristic complaint is, "I haven't the time"; for an age whose economy demands constantly improved efficiency, which means less time for the same amount of production; for an age that rushes through the week to reach the weekend and then rushes through the weekend to rush through another week to reach the weekend. . . . For such an age the word "wait" is a wise word. For why do we hurry? Where are we going in such a rush?

You can't rush God certainly. He doesn't seem to be in a hurry. And unless we slow down and wait for him occasionally, we may miss him entirely in our frenzied rushing about. It was to Simeon, you remember, "waiting for the consolation of Israel," that our Lord appeared. And he appeared not only to Simeon but to the world "in the fullness of time," which is simply another way of saying that you can't rush God.

Is it not significant for an age in a hurry that it's the

devil in the New Testament who is always trying to rush things? At the very start of Christ's ministry it was the devil who came there in the wilderness with his suggestion to step up God's tempo. "Get going," he said, "You haven't much time! Turn stones into bread! Cast yourself down from the temple! Bow down and worship me! For I have the secret for an age in a hurry." No question about it, the devil is shrewd. He knows the attraction for an age in a hurry of cutting corners, of crowd appeal, of signs and wonders. He knows our distaste for the long slow road of suffering love and death. Time and again our Lord had to face this same devilish desire to rush God. Recall the aftermath to the feeding of the five thousand when they came and wanted to fix things up in a hurry by making this rabbi who could fill their stomachs so miraculously their king, or when the disciples wanted to fix things up in a hurry by calling God's judgment of fire down upon an inhospitable village. The devil is shrewd because he knows that if you stop and wait on the Lord for a moment, you may discover what the devil's up to.

But our Lord knew that God won't be hurried. For what is this urge to rush God but an effort to bend God's will to ours, rather than the other way around? Think for a moment. Take that minute you're "losing" now to ask a question. When is it that you become impatient with God? Is it not almost invariably a time when he doesn't act the way we think he ought to act? When he doesn't answer prayer the way we want it answered? When we take matters into our own hands and then wonder why he doesn't step in promptly and clean up the mess we've made? Chances are that when we grow impatient with God it's because we can't get him to do things our way, the way we think any self-respecting God ought to handle things!

But how shall we ever know him or his will unless we "wait on the Lord"? Stop this mad scramble to save a minute, and lose the minute to place ourselves quietly and humbly before him in prayer, filling that minute not with our hot and hasty demands and desires, but with a search for his! Then, perhaps, we'll catch something of the wonder of his patience with us. Then, perhaps, we'll begin to understand that the patience of God, that which makes us most impatient with him, that utterly maddening patience of his, is the most remarkable evidence of his love for us. For suppose he did step in all hot and breathless like some of our prayers and ruthlessly root out the evil in the world, what would be left? Of you? Of me? How incomprehensible is this amazing patience of his which will suffer our harried pettiness and our frantic indifference to him and then at the end of the day be ready, once again, to hear our prayers of contrition and remorse for all our hurried failures and stupidities and—wonder of wonders!—be willing to accept them!

What other response, then, can we give to such a God but to wait . . . wait patiently for him? For you and I know full well that some things in life, usually the best things, will not be hurried. The flash of inspiration which results in a great poem, a deathless piece of music, or the design for a magnificent building, is deceptive. The flash of inspiration conceals the years of discipline, of drudgery and study, of just plain grinding work, without which the flash of inspiration would never have come. Waiting for the flash of inspiration came first, sometimes years of it.

Nor can the growth from childhood to maturity be hurried. Have you ever noticed that Jesus was no upstart child prodigy? We make much of the twelve-year-old talking with learned theologians in the temple. Perhaps we make too much of it. For over against that one incident are almost thirty years of which we know nothing, thirty years of slow growth and preparation and waiting before he flashed across the stage of the world's history. Today I suppose we'd call him a "late bloomer"!

Nor can the knowledge of God be hurried. I suspect that most of our difficulties in school and college with the problem of the existence of God result from a desire for quick answers. I know it was true in my own case. I threw it all overboard because I wanted answers fast: at the end of the first semester of my sophomore year, let us say.

But if God's plan for us is to win us to love and trust in him, can love be hurried? Can trust be won overnight? "Lose a minute, save a life . . . for the life you save may be your own." Faith is not faith until it is willing to stop in its mad rush in order to "wait on the Lord," and to accept the marvelous patience of God with us.

But must we always exercise the same patience? Is "wait" the only word for our time? What of the urgency behind Paul's admonitions, "You know what hour it is . . . high time to wake out of sleep. . . . The night is far spent the day is at hand. . . . See then that ye walk circumspectly, not as fools but as wise, redeeming the time . . ."? Wisdom here seems to be coupled not with waiting at all but with a sense of hurry up because time and tide wait for no man! Probe the original behind that word "time" and you come up with "fit time" or "opportunity." It suggests that we'd better hurry because God won't wait! If God is unbelievably patient with us, it appears that God can be unbelievably impatient with us, too!

The dilemma here, which marks one of the central paradoxes in biblical thought, does not seem quite so perplexing if we look again at the life of our Lord. If Christ knew the value of "wait" in the face of the devilish suggestion to push God and his will around in a hurry, he did not take his eternity either. I am growing increasingly impatient with portrayals of Christ on film. Possibly you have seen some of these films where Christ is always pictured as never in a hurry, always pacing slowly through the countryside as if he were walking in a perpetual ecclesiastical procession. But is this accurate? I recall one vivid scene which Mark pictures for us with Jesus striding on ahead on the way up to Jerusalem and the disciples following on behind "amazed" and "afraid." You can't miss the quick decisiveness in our Lord's stride nor the picture of the disciples scurrying after him unable to keep up with his stride or his spirit!

It's clear, then, that waiting for the Lord is not like waiting at the airport for a plane to arrive, standing around twiddling our thumbs or idly leafing through a magazine to "kill time." Waiting for the Lord is more like a youngster waiting to grow up. Each moment, each day has its own opportunities which are to be seized, for each moment, each opportunity seized is in fact the moment of growing to maturity.

So with God and his will for us. We wait for the Lord knowing that God will not be hurried into any little plans or schemes of ours. But if we wait with minds and hearts alert, each moment presents us with the opportunity to bend our will to his, to "redeem the time" by opening ourselves to his love.

I know that sometimes it seems that Christians hear only the word to wait and, misunderstanding the word, take their eternity to face crucial issues. There are those who caution us only to wait when the unity of the church is mentioned, reminding us of the great and fundamental truth—and it *is* a great and fundamental truth—that unity is a gift and cannot be hurried by any frantic organizational schemes of ours. But to others it seems as if some churches were only taking their eternity to face the issue.

There are also thoroughly devout and sincere Christians who hear only the word to wait when anything regarding the racial problem comes up. As a result the church for the most part has been taking its eternity while professional sports, schools, public accommodations, the armed forces, and even public housing redeem the time. The difficulty here is that the wise admonition to wait may blind us to the "fit time," the opportunity, because the time never seems to us to be quite "fit."

And yet the only time we have in the sight of God is now. "Now is the accepted time; now is the day of salvation." Waiting for the Lord does not mean waiting for tomorrow, for tomorrow never comes. It's always today. Waiting for the Lord means recognizing that God will not be hurried or forced into our little plans and schemes. That's true. But waiting for the Lord also means that we will approach each moment expectantly, knowing that in each "now" God places before us the opportunity for trust and obedience.

This is not to be interpreted, as some are prone to do, that everything that happens, happens because God wills it, so that "waiting for the Lord" becomes a matter of submitting as gracefully as possible to what is called the "inscrutable will of God," which all too often turns out to be a thinly disguised fatalism; what is to be is to be. On the contrary, we are free agents, not puppets, free to thumb our collective noses at God if we've a mind to, and to twist his will and purpose into the horror of a Harlem slum, a Belsen and a Buchenwald, or into a vast nuclear devastation. "Waiting for the Lord," consequently, is not meek and inert resignation. "Faith in providence," as another has put it, "affirms . . . that God is living and active in that which happens, that God has resources sufficient for all emergencies, and that the sovereignty of his care is revealed by his ability to turn evil into good."[1] Thus, though God does not will everything that happens, he does will something *in* everything that happens. So we "wait" in order to discern that will, and "hurry" lest the divine opportunity in each moment pass us by.

Consequently that prayer, "Make haste, O God, to help me," which sounds so appropriate for an age in a rush, does not mean that God is lagging behind somewhere and we are urging him to catch up with our eager, liberated, and impatient spirits. God is already there ahead of us in each moment, in each here and now, impatiently waiting for us. So we pray, "Make haste, O God, to help me," lest we rush on by and miss the comfort and claim of his presence which is available to us only here and only now.

[1] Gustaf Aulén, *The Faith of the Christian Church* (Philadelphia: Muhlenberg, 1948), p. 200.

149

I have a little book of daily devotions entitled, "God's Minute." The title is utterly misleading, a bit of pious sentimentality, because it suggests that only the minute spent in conscious prayer or devotion is "God's minute." But every minute is God's minute because every minute in God's eyes is always now. "See then that ye walk circumspectly, not as fools but as wise, redeeming the 'now.'" For God is there waiting for you and your life may be hanging in the balance.

So the twin admonitions which seem so contradictory: Wait . . . Hurry; Hurry . . . Wait. Both are true and not one after another or one at one time and the other on another occasion, but both together and at the same time. For wait is the expression of faith, of openness; hurry is the expression of obedience; together they spell faithful, trusting obedience, the creaturely response to the God who created him.

If we overemphasize the "hurry," the result is a crisis theology that is breathless and frenetic and an ethic that goes off at loose ends and winds up in legalism. If we overemphasize the "wait," the result is a lacklustre passivity which sits by while the world, the flesh, and the devil redeem the time. But taken together and at the same moment, "wait" . . . "hurry" . . . describe the creaturely response to the God who made us and gives his all for us. So we seize the moment in obedience to God's will of love now, trusting in that same moment that we may discern his will and that that same will of forgiving love will be done to us as well as through us.

Wait . . . Hurry!

The Feeling and the Reality

As a hart longs for flowing streams,
so longs my soul for thee, O God.
My soul thirsts for God, for the living God.
When shall I come and behold the face of God?
My tears have been my food day and night,
while men say to me continually, "Where is your God?"

These things I remember, as I pour out my soul:
how I went with the throng, and led them in procession to
the house of God,
with glad shouts and songs of thanksgiving, a multitude keeping festival.
Why are you cast down, O my soul, and why are you disquieted within me?
Hope in God; for I shall again praise him, my help and my
God.

My soul is cast down within me, therefore I remember thee
from the land of Jordan and of Hermon, from Mount Mizar.
Deep calls to deep at the thunder of thy cataracts;
all thy waves and thy billows have gone over me.
By day the Lord commands his steadfast love; and at night
his song is with me, a prayer to the God of my life.

I say to God, my rock; "Why hast thou forgotten me?
Why go I mourning because of the oppression of the enemy?"
As with a deadly wound in my body, my adversaries taunt me,
while they say to me continually, "Where is your God?"

Why are you cast down, O my soul, and why are you dis-
quieted within me?
Hope in God; for I shall again praise him, my help and my
God.   *—Psalm 42*

Life has its ups and downs. No observation about human life and experience is more trite, more obvious. There
are good days and bad days, times when everything seems
to go well and times when everything seems to go wrong,
sunshine and rain, joy and sorrow. We all recognize this
and any comment upon it would seem superfluous.

And yet when it comes to the recognition and awareness of God's reality, power, and presence, there seems to
be a widespread misunderstanding that in this area, the
normal ups and downs of life do not apply. I was talking
with some college students not too long ago and when I
indicated that the presence of doubts and misgivings about
God's reality and presence was a normal part of religious
experience they acted as if they had never heard of this
possibility before. They simply assumed that if a person
were deeply religious, a fully committed Christian, as we
say, there would be no doubts or questions, no dark days,
no fits of depression, no ups and downs. And if you did
have these fits of depression, these dark hours of wondering and questioning, it simply meant that you were not as
"religious," as "committed," as you ought to be.

But the record of man's experience of God as it comes
down to us through the pages of the Bible is full of the
downs as well as the ups. The Psalms, for example, that
book of great devotional literature, a kind of mirror re-

flecting the total religious experience of the ancient Jews, is faithful in reflecting the low moments as well as the high moments of faith and assurance. It speaks of God's face being "turned away," of his being "afar off," of his "forgetting me," of dark hours when there is no voice, no sign of God's presence and concern: "How long wilt thou forget me, O God, forever?" "I am weary of my crying, my throat is parched while I wait for my God."

Or if you turn to the New Testament, you find Paul, the great apostle of faith, with his "thorn," praying desperately that it be removed. But it's not removed. Even the experience of our Lord reflects the same moments of darkness and apparent abandonment. The story of the temptation in the wilderness at the beginning of his ministry is undoubtedly a picture of the struggle which went on throughout his life and points to long periods when the only voice he heard was not the voice of God at all but the voice of the tempter—the dark questions about himself, his destiny, his God. Moreover, the struggle in the garden the night before he died and the cry of dereliction on the cross, "My God, why hast thou forsaken me, why art thou so far from helping me?" accent the same moments of darkness.

All this should be reassuring to us when we experience the inevitable downs in life, those moments when God seems far off and unreal, even a vast mockery. At least we can know that the great saints of the past and even our Lord himself went through the same dry periods of darkness and depression. It's not an uncommon experience at all even for the most deeply religious people that the ups and downs of life are to be expected as a normal part of our sense of awareness of the presence and power and love of God.

But the practical question remains: How shall we manage when these dark hours, these moods of depression come? The forty-second Psalm is a remarkably faithful and accurate record of just this experience so common to all of us and may, therefore, provide some clues.

It begins with the familiar experience of the dry periods when God seems far off and unconcerned: "As the hart panteth after the water brooks, so panteth my soul after thee, O God. My soul thirsts for God, the living God. When shall I come and behold the face of God?"

The Psalmist then records the mockery which so often accompanies these moods of depression: "My tears have been my food day and night, while men say to me continually, 'Where is your God?' " . . . as if people were actually laughing at us and taunting us for even hoping that there might be a God who really cares what happens to us. For it is characteristic of these dark hours that not only does God seem not to care a rap, but everybody else seems to be against us too—or at least unable to understand our situation. Later on he speaks of them quite accurately as "enemies" and "adversaries": "Why go I mourning because of the oppression of the enemy? As with a deadly wound in my body my adversaries taunt me while they say to me continually, 'Where is your God?' " Who among us has not known this feeling and seen it in others? When you attempt to comfort or reassure, they react as if no one could possibly understand or help; everyone becomes an "enemy" or an "adversary"; our efforts to encourage, sympathize, or cheer seem to be nothing but a mockery. Even now you may be thinking, "What does this preacher know about *my* life, *my* problems, *my* moments of darkness and depression? It's all well and good for him to talk, but if he were in my shoes. . . ." So the preacher too becomes an "adversary," an "enemy."

The Psalmist is accurate, too, in recording these moods as coming in waves; for the Psalm itself moves back and forth from depression to reassurance to depression and back to reassurance again. For right after he gives expression to hope and faith, he immediately falls back into the fit of depression again: "My soul is cast down within me." And this is faithful to our experience too. For normally these feelings of darkness and abandonment come over us in waves, alternating with brighter moments of hope and reassurance.

I think we can therefore trust this unknown poet of the ancient past because he obviously knows what these dry, dark periods of ours are really like. But now where does he get his reassurance in the middle of the darkness?

The first thing he does is to call to remembrance those brighter hours in the past when God did seem to be close and concerned: "These things I remember as I pour out my soul; How I went with the throng and led them in procession to the house of God with glad shouts and songs of thanksgiving." Apparently there had been days when the tide of faith was running strong and God had been very much alive for him and he had entered into a festive procession to give thanks and praise to God, much as you and I have gone to church on Christmas or Easter with high and expectant hearts. And it was days like these which he called to mind when he was depressed.

This obviously suggests that we need to emphasize the importance of memory in our experience of God. We are not concerned here with God as some shadowy ideal, the projection of a man's happier and more confident hours and consequently a God whose reality fades as our consciousness of him fades. We are concerned here with a God who acts in history, the history of the world and your individual history and mine. And so Christian worship is always concerned in large part simply with remembering how God has acted in the past—for if he truly is God, then this must be the way that he always acts. This is why the recital of the Creed, the reading of Scripture, the use of the Psalms, the preaching on a passage of the Bible, the participation in the Sacrament of the Altar, are the indispensable and most prominent parts of Christian worship to which we give our response in prayer and praise.

Bishop Hanns Lilje of Germany tells of the dark days when the Nazis had thrown him into prison and had stripped him of all his possessions including even his Bible.[1] All he had left for his prayers and meditations and the reassurance that God still cared were the things he remembered in Scripture and prayer in days now past which once had been bright with assurance, promise, and hope. And the things he remembered helped him through the dark hours when there seemed to be no possible future except a brief imprisonment followed swiftly by violent death at the hands of a firing squad.

The same thing in less dramatic form is also true of us. When we repeat the twenty-third Psalm in days of depres-

[1] Hanns Lilje, *The Valley of the Shadow* (Philadelphia: Muhlenberg, 1950), p. 55.

sion and loneliness and doubt and grief, as a kind of last-ditch prayer of desperation, "The Lord is my shepherd. . . ," those familiar words, probably committed to memory as a child, are reinforced in that dark hour by the times when we repeated them when there was no question or doubt in our minds. Memory helps us to see our present situation in some kind of perspective. For you will notice that the Psalmist here recognizes that although the feeling of depression is perfectly genuine, it is still a feeling and not necessarily the clue to the reality of the situation.

This is why from remembering the brighter days in the past he turns not to the present but to an affirmation of confidence in the future: "Why art thou cast down, O my soul, and why art thou disquieted within me? Hope in God for I shall again praise him." I like the down-to-earth frankness of this ancient poet. There's no pious attempt to fool himself that the feeling of depression and loneliness isn't there. It is. Nor is there any equally pious attempt to force himself into a different kind of feeling of God's presence and reality, asking God to give him a "meaningful worship experience," for example! It's as if he were saying, "Look, I'm in the dumps now. There's no laughing it off or pretending that God seems real when he doesn't. But this feeling I have is no sure clue to the reality behind the situation. I do remember times when God was near and real for me, and because of God's unchanging faithfulness I know there will come a time when I will again praise him even though I have no stomach for it now. That's the reality behind the feeling to which I cling. Therefore, why art thou cast down, O my soul? . . . Hope thou in God!"

One evening I was listening to a fervent preacher exhorting his congregation to have a "feeling" for God's presence and reality. "Feel it," he said, "and then you're sure you have it." I can sympathize with a preacher's desire to create a feeling of warmth and certainty in a cold and uncertain world. But what he said couldn't have been farther from the experience reflected in this Psalm. Here the feeling is certainly not the clue to the reality of God. It rarely is. God is God whether we happen to feel that he is God or not. And it is precisely when we don't feel the reality of God's presence that we need the assurance of his reality the most. So here, even when this man is giving vent to his feeling of darkness and depression, he calls God his "rock": "I say to God, my rock, why hast thou forgotten me?" He certainly didn't *feel* as if God were his rock at the moment! This was rather an expression of faith in God's unchanging reality right in the middle of the shifting sands of his feelings and emotions.

This is certainly not to say that there is no validity to the experience of God which affects our feelings and emotions. A religion devoid of emotion is like cold beef stew, a tasteless and perverted thing. But it is to say that our emotions, our feelings about God, are not the court of last resort. As a matter of fact they are pretty treacherous when it comes to an assurance of God's unchanging presence and care. Far better to reflect the wisdom of the Psalmist who, without soft-pedaling the feeling of despondency and despair, nevertheless found assurance of God's constancy in his remembrance of the past and on that basis made his declaration of faith concerning the future: "I will again praise him, my help and my God."

"Why hast thou forgotten me?" That's the feeling. And it comes to all of us, even to the most devout and dedicated and committed. But the feeling is not the reality. "My rock . . . my help, my God"—that's the reality, God unchanging in his faithfulness regardless of the way I happen to feel at the moment.

Whenever these dark hours come, and they do come to every last one of us at one time or another, may I suggest that you turn to this forty-second Psalm. You'll not find a more accurate reflection of your own dark experience— and the answer to it—anywhere. And perhaps you too will come out at the end of it to say with him, "Why art thou cast down, O my soul, and why art thou disquieted within me? Hope thou in God; for I shall again praise him, my help and my God."

Is God as Good as Jesus?

Now when John heard in prison about the deeds of the Christ, he sent word by his disciples and said to him, "Are you he who is to come, or shall we look for another?" And Jesus answered them, "Go and tell John what you hear and see: the blind receive their sight and the lame walk, lepers are cleansed and the deaf hear, and the dead are raised up, and the poor have good news preached to them. And blessed is he who takes no offense at me."   —*Matthew 11:2-6*

Philip said to him, "Lord, show us the Father, and we shall be satisfied." Jesus said to him, "Have I been with you so long, and yet you do not know me, Philip? He who has seen me has seen the Father; how can you say, 'Show us the Father'? Do you not believe that I am in the Father and the Father in me? The words that I say to you I do not speak on my own authority; but the Father who dwells in me does his works. Believe me that I am in the Father and the Father in me; or else believe me for the sake of the works themselves."   —*John 14:8-11*

Is God as good as Jesus? The question may seem a little strange at first but it is an actual question put to me in an agony of spirit by a man who spent a number of years in the Far East. He told me how he had been torn apart at the sight of unbelievable mass misery: the hundreds upon hundreds of thousands of people living in abject poverty, racked by disease, half-starved, illiterate. And for

160

most of them—and this was the damnable part of it—absolutely nothing to look forward to in the future that would offer anything but the same kind of grinding misery. Over here, he said, in our pleasant churches and surrounded for the most part by good, decent people, it's relatively easy to believe that God is good, even granting the poverty and suffering and injustice so many people have to endure even in America. But considering these masses of people in Asia who have known nothing but poverty and disease and can look forward in this life to nothing more, "I wish," he said, "I wish I could believe that God is as good as Jesus."

You and I may not have had precisely that kind of experience, although I don't see how any one of us who lives in a large city can avoid it in the face of the hopeless filth, rats, and poverty of our slums. Surely the question has bothered us too on more than one occasion, and particulary at the sudden onset of tragic suffering. How is it possible to believe in a good God in a world like this? Is it actually possible that God—by whatever name we call him, fate, the mysterious power behind the universe, life principle, ground of being—can actually be as good as Jesus?

The question is not new, of course. It has plagued the minds of men even back when Jesus walked the earth. Then too the question arose: This Jesus is a good man but is God—the Very God—actually like this man, Jesus?

John the Baptist raised the question after he had been put in prison. And as he looked out of his prison cell at a world with evil running amok, and at Jesus talking about love and forgiveness and apparently doing nothing about the evil except forgiving it, the bitterness welled up inside of him. Although he had welcomed Jesus earlier as God's own emissary who would bring the kingdom of God to earth, now he could stand the doubts no longer and so he sent a delegation of his followers to Jesus with the question, "Are you really the promised one of God— or should we look somewhere else?" For John, it was this same question: Does God actually act like this Jesus of Nazareth?

Later on it was Philip who raised the question. Philip had had the advantage of being one of the disciples. He had enjoyed the companionship of Jesus throughout his ministry. And yet along toward the end, just before the crucifixion, Philip raised the same basic question: "Lord, show us the Father and we shall be satisfied." In other words, "Lord, we've lived with you, listened to you and watched you, and it's all been amazingly wonderful. But now tell us frankly, candidly, just what is God actually like. Lord, show us the Father. . . ." Jesus' reply only underlines the unrecognized pathos behind the question, "Have I been so long with you, and yet you do not know me, Philip?"

That same reply could have been given to my friend, for he too had been a devoted churchman all his life and had come to know Jesus intimately down through the years. And yet he, like Philip, was at least honest enough to raise the question openly.

For there is a dangerous tendency, particularly in days like these, to avoid the question. When the world looks increasingly like an insoluble mess: communist infiltration in Africa, China and the nuclear bomb, the Congo, Cuba,

Vietnam; or, closer to home, a social revolution festering just below the surface, waiting perhaps only for warmer weather to erupt into violence again; then it can be an easy matter to retreat into a church and worship Christ, the good, the gentle, the loving figure on a cross, without raising the sticky question whether God—the God of the world outside the church—is actually like that.

So even if suffering and the madness of these days may not have forced the question on you, for the good of our souls and the depth of our convictions, we'd better face it.

And let's begin by asking another question. If God is not as good as Jesus, then just what kind of God do we expect him to be? It's perfectly clear what kind of God John the Baptist was looking for, a God who would use his power to stamp out evil. For he had said of the coming of Jesus at the beginning of his ministry, "Even now the ax is laid to the root of the trees; every tree therefore that does not bear good fruit is cut down and thrown into the fire" (Matt. 3:10).

And I suppose a lot of people today would share John's feelings. Why does God—if he's both good and powerful—let evil get away with what it does in our world? Why doesn't he step in and simply stamp it out? Do away with the Castros and Mao Tse Tungs, to say nothing of the gangsters, narcotics peddlers, and vicious delinquents at home? Many of our deep resentments directed against what we call rabble rousers of whatever color or stripe, whether we think of them in terms of John Birchers or White Citizen Councils or NAACP's or woolly-headed liberals or Communists or black reactionaries, are actually an unrecognized desire like that of John for God to step in and stamp out the evil ones in the world, or at least to shut them up!

And the answer to that is still another question. Where would he stop? Where would he stop if he were to step in and crush all the greed and lust for power and pride and selfishness and inhumanity, all the common, tawdry evil and indifference which breeds further evil? Would he stop with me perhaps? Or with you? Who would be left among us to enjoy this fair world if all evil were to be stamped out and thrown into the fire? We're always tempted to forget that the evil which crucified the good Jesus was not found among gangsters, narcotics pushers, and delinquents, but among the good, pious, religious people of the day, people precisely like you and me. John the Baptist forgot all this too, I suspect, that even he would not have been spared to see the evil cast into the fire.

When you come to Philip, I suppose the kind of God he was looking for was a God who would give visible and tangible proof that he was around: through a vision perhaps, or in a burning bush, or in a pillar of cloud by day and a pillar of fire by night. It's the same old itch for signs and wonders. Philip had seen the wonders of our Lord's life, but these apparently were not enough; there was always a question mark left at the end. You always need a second miracle to prove that the first was not a coincidence.

But how can you prove love? How could a God of love prove beyond the shadow of a doubt his love for you? If he would answer just this one prayer! But tomorrow or the next day there'd be another problem, another prayer, and the demand for another proof of his love. Actually there can be no proof that God is as good as Jesus. There can be no proof for any of the deep involvements in life. The love of a man for a woman or of a mother for her child—how can you prove that? Indeed, to demand the proof is to deny the love. And so what could Jesus say to Philip but, "Have I been so long with you, Philip, and yet you do not know me?" No miracles, no signs and wonders, no "proof" could be offered beyond what he had already shown himself to be.

When, therefore, we ask ourselves the question, what kind of God are you looking for, this doesn't answer the question whether God is as good as Jesus, but it begins to bring the question into sharper focus. Are we really so sure we know how God *ought* to act if he were as good as Jesus?

And perhaps we'd better examine that word "good" for a moment, too. I suppose we mean by it that Jesus went about helping people, getting them out of trouble, curing their diseases, feeding them when they were hungry, being gentle and kind, and in the end giving his life for them. And all this is true, of course, but it's not the whole picture. Have you ever thought of all the cripples and lepers and mentally ill in Palestine that Jesus did *not* cure even though presumably he could have? It's a harsh way of putting it, but the fact remains that his major mission was not simply that of making life more comfortable or even to ease suffering.

To complete the picture of our Lord's "goodness," we have to remember too the demands he made upon people: "Let the dead bury their dead and come follow me. . . . Hard is the way and narrow is the gate that leads to life and few there be who find it. . . . If any man would come after me, let him deny himself and take up his cross. . . ." No, when we ask whether God is as good as Jesus, we have to remember all that Jesus said and was, not just the parts of his life we like to remember. Otherwise the question becomes sentimental.

But often enough the question isn't sentimental at all because it arises out of a man's own agony or out of the agony of watching others suffer, when life seems to make no sense at all on the basis of a good and loving God, and the question is wrenched out of us, Why? Why, if there's a loving God, does he let it go on? It is reported that Dag Hammarskjold's sister put a wreath on his grave with one word written across it, "Why?"

There is no easy answer. And I am reticent to say very much at this point because I know that others, no doubt some of you, have suffered far more than I can imagine. With that deeply felt acknowledgement, let me offer one or two brief hints which will certainly not solve the problem, but may perhaps help us to understand it a little better.

First, much of the suffering on earth is caught up in the mystery of human freedom and responsibility. We are created in the image of God, and that means as free, responsible men. God's love for us respects that freedom and responsibility. He will not treat us as puppets on a string, even when we want him to, even when we make a mess of our lives or when others make a mess of life around us; even when we really wish he would refuse to treat us as sons and treat us as puppets instead, relieve us of the necessity of difficult decision or of self-discipline, get us or those we love out of the mess by some miracle or other. But he will not manipulate us into doing what he wants done even when it is obviously for our own good. We are made in his image, free, responsible creatures, and his love for us respects that freedom and responsibility even when innocent bystanders get hurt. It's hard to accept because it's hard to be a free, responsible child and not a puppet. But there it is.

Second, much of the suffering around us is involved in the risks we take when we let ourselves love someone else. The chances of getting hurt are simply multiplied to the degree we let ourselves get involved in the lives of others. If we have children, we open ourselves to the joys of family life, of course, but we also open ourselves to the hurt that others may do to them and to the hurt they may do to us and to the pain of losing them eventually.

So on a vaster scale, the closer our world is brought together through technology and communications and increasing population, the more possibilities there are that we will get hurt. And so more people than we suspect withdraw from love, from involvement in the lives of others, not because they are cold or unfeeling necessarily, but because they cannot stand the risk of getting hurt which is the risk of involvement in the lives of other human beings.

But if Jesus was right, this is precisely what God intended, that we were created in community for community together. So long as anyone in the community suffers, everyone suffers. But again, if Jesus is our standard of how we think God ought to act, then he did identify himself with us in love so that all our sufferings became his.

God knows what it's like, for he is in it with you. God knows what it's like to be you!

There is no easy answer to the problem of suffering or to the question whether God is really as good as Jesus. The answer Jesus gave to John the Baptist and to Philip was essentially the same: I can't prove it to you but look at what I am and what I am doing and come to your own decision.

And so it comes down to this, in the end, a man simply has to choose:

On the one hand here is this mass of human suffering and misery, the terrifying mystery of evil in the world and in ourselves, the senseless waste of human resources in mental institutions, the still-born children, the multiple sclerosis and cancer, the savage wreckage of flood and earthquake and war and delinquency and poverty . . . and a man can conclude that none of it makes any sense; there is no God at all and if there is, he's a monster.

Or, on the other hand, you have this deathless picture of a man, caught in the same world, faced with the same evil, who wept over his beloved Jerusalem and at the grave of his friend, who felt the torturing doubt in the garden, "Good God, is there no other way?" Who knew the abyss of despair, "My God, why . . . ?" Here was no phantom deity moving through life untouched by the agonizing questions which tear us apart, and yet he spent his life and suffered his agonies and died his death—not that we might think that *he* was good . . . remember? "Why call ye me good?" . . . but only so that you and I might know that in and behind and beyond this world there is this mysterious One whom we may call—incredibly—"Father." One whose only will for us and for our world is love; whose power can be expressed only in love. "He that hath seen me," Jesus said to Philip, "hath seen the Father."

A man must choose. A barren, brassy sky with nothing —or with a monster. Or, "Father." But those who have made this second choice, that God is as good as Jesus, know a confidence that no suffering or evil on earth can destroy. It can shake it, heaven knows! But it cannot destroy it. For they can say with Paul, "I am persuaded that neither death nor life, nor angels nor principalities nor powers, nor things present nor things to come nor height nor depth nor any other creature shall be able to separate us—not from the love of Christ!—but from the love of God which is in Christ Jesus our Lord."

Strangers and Pilgrims

These all died in faith, not having received what was promised, but having seen it and greeted it from afar, and having
acknowledged that they were strangers and exiles on the earth.
For people who speak thus make it clear that they are seeking a homeland. If they had been thinking of that land from
which they had gone out, they would have had opportunity to
return. But as it is, they desire a better country, that is, a
heavenly one. Therefore God is not ashamed to be called
their God, for he has prepared for them a city.

—Hebrews 11:13-16

"Strangers and exiles"—so an unknown writer character-
izes the great men of faith in the Old Testament wandering about looking for a homeland. "These all died in
faith . . . having acknowledged that they were strangers
and exiles on the earth." But these words "strangers and
exiles" are not simply words out of a dim and dusty past.
They have appeared as almost daily items in every newspaper in the past twenty-five years. They are a grim and
factual description of literally millions of our contempo-
raries.

Leon Uris has made this shockingly clear in his slash-
ing novel, *Exodus,* a story of the pogroms and more subtle
persecutions carried on against the Jews in our time. But
it is not the Jews only who are "strangers and exiles."
Recall the boatloads of DP's from the Baltic states and

Germany in the forties and in more recent days the Chinese in Hong Kong, the Arabs in Palestine, the Cubans in Florida, the Puerto Ricans in New York City, the East Germans once flooding and now trickling into West Berlin whether by tunnel or by a truck sent crashing through the wall.

But a man does not have to be driven from his homeland—though that is tragic enough—to be a stranger and an exile. The fires of nationalism now burning in Africa are fed by a refusal to be "strangers and exiles" in the very lands where they, their fathers and forefathers, have lived for generations. And the Negroes in our own country are understandably fed up with a hundred years and more of waiting to be recognized as something more than "strangers and exiles" in the United States of America. All of which may provide a clue to the deeper meaning of these haunting words.

For all of us are "strangers and exiles" no matter what the color of the skin and no matter where we happen to live on this earth. C. S. Lewis calls it the "inconsolable secret" in each one of us, our "sense of exile on earth as it is . . . the sense that in this universe we are treated as strangers. . . ." He goes on, ". . . at present we are on the outside of the world, the wrong side of the door. We discern the freshness and purity of morning, but they do not make us fresh and pure. We cannot mingle with the splendours we see!"[1] Is it not so? Else why does beautiful music bring tears to our eyes? We say we were "deeply moved"; but moved to what? To an intense longing to

[1] C. S. Lewis, *The Weight of Glory* (New York: Macmillan, 1949), pp. 5, 11, 13.

"get inside" the beauty of the music perhaps? Why are our moments of greatest happiness edged with tears? Why is it that we "weep for joy"?

The inconsolable secret is that we *are* "strangers and exiles" on this earth. And so we try every conceivable device to deny the secret and ease the pain. Some attempt to dull the pain with the obvious sedatives: TV, the corner bar, or the comforting sensation of rubbing our fur against the fur of other human animals. Adolescents, for whom the sudden awakening to the fact that they are indeed "strangers and exiles" is all but unbearable, characteristically pull themselves into all sorts of queer shapes to prove to themselves and to their peers that this is the one thing they are not, that they're completely, utterly, even bitterly at home in their world and ours. And a lot of us never outgrow this adolescent reaction. We think we can overcome the sense of exile and estrangement by proving to ourselves and to those around us that we *are* at home here. And so we build our little fortresses of financial security, cultivate a cordon of friends, throw ourselves into community projects, keep up with the latest jargon—whether it's modern art, recent recordings, contemporary theology, or foreign sports cars; learn to shop at the shops where people in the know presumably shop—all this and more so that nobody will guess, not even ourselves, the root of the inconsolable secret, that we're really not at home in our world, that we're strangers and exiles on this earth.

But men of faith have always known that they were "strangers and exiles." The thing that sets them apart is that they've known it and it hasn't bothered them! "These all died in faith . . . having *acknowledged* that they were strangers and exiles on this earth." One of the earliest names for the followers of Jesus was "those of the Way." They were people who knew that they were not permanent residents here. So the word "exiles" is sometimes translated "pilgrims," or as the New English Bible has it, "passing travelers," and the phrase becomes "strangers and pilgrims." Like the ancient Jews wandering through the wilderness in search of a promised land, Christians have always known themselves to be passing travelers, "strangers and pilgrims" of the Way. And when they settled down temporarily they became a "parish." The word "parish," as William Barclay reminds us, comes from a Greek word meaning a "body of aliens in the midst of any community,"[2] not, as we have sometimes come to think of a parish, an innocuous group of like-minded idealists—or conformists or hypocrites, depending on the point of view.

Now, to be sure, this acknowledgment of our fundamental situation as strangers and pilgrims, a parish of aliens, has frequently been distorted. Some have thought it means that we must deny the world we live in as an unhappy vale of tears simply to be endured, or as an evil world from which the pious Christian should withdraw, whether totally in monastery and convent, or partially by drawing the line at such "worldly" pursuits as the theatre, dancing, smoking, and drinking, or by shunning barber shops and dressmakers.

But this denial of the world is not what is meant by the acknowledgment that we are strangers and pilgrims. Our

[2] William Barclay, *A New Testament Wordbook* (Chicago: SCM Book Club, 1955), p. 125.

Lord did not deny the world, its pleasures or its tragedies. He "came eating and drinking," and took delight in banquets and wedding receptions, and multiplied the supply of wine when it ran low, and—misunderstood—was called a "winebibber and a glutton." Or, on another occasion, he stood at the grave of a friend and wept. No one so identified himself with life around him in all its infinite variety of pleasures and pains, and yet his kingdom was not of this world! He was strangely at home even on a cross!

The point, you see, is that our Lord and those who followed him in faith were not frustrated by the obvious fact that this world is not our permanent home. They neither denied the world and fled from it nor were they taken captive by it. Because they were not strangers and exiles at the center of life, in their relationship to God, they found themselves curiously at home in a world which they gladly acknowledged was not their permanent residence.

Someone has suggested that our stay here on earth is like a traveler stopping at an inn—and a very splendid one at that. Anyone who has ever stayed at a good inn or hotel knows that it can be a delightful experience to the degree that it is recognized as not being a permanent home. You can explore the rooms, lounges, and gardens, enjoy the delights of maid service and good food, enter into the fascinations of its shops and activities. But nothing can be lonelier than that same inn if there is no other home to which you can return.

So with life here on earth. Somewhere along the line in this "age of anxiety" we have lost sight of the fact that we are passing travelers along the way, "strangers and pilgrims," stopping briefly at a delightful and frequently perplexing inn. Consequently we can't understand why we should feel so anxious and lonely. Our desperate efforts to "adjust" to life around us, to set up our little securities of family and fortune only serve to increase the anxiety and loneliness, for we are hopelessly attempting to transform an inn for transients into a permanent home. And our hearts secretly rebel, for they are stubbornly restless until they find their rest in a homeland only God can provide.

But once we acknowledge this world for the inn along the side of the road that it really is, then we too can find ourselves curiously at home here. This is a clue to a number of puzzling passages in the New Testament.

On the one hand, some of our Lord's almost savage-sounding statements become clear. When he says, for example, that unless a man "hate his father and mother and wife and children . . . he cannot be my disciple," this sounds callous and brutal and destructive of life's basic community, the family, which even he used as an analogy for the kingdom of God. But what he is actually saying here is that even the most sacred and permanent relationships here on earth—including the love of a family—can become demonic if we try to make them ultimately permanent. For we are essentially "strangers and pilgrims" with respect to our families too, as every child must come to learn before he gets very far along in life, and as I have found necessary to learn all over again only recently as the children grow up and move out. Nothing can give more sheer delight than the bonds of marriage and a family if they are acknowledged as belonging only to the transient and the passing. But let a mother or a child find her ultimate home only in the human family and the inevitable result is deepened anxiety and frustration, the warped and twisted child whose parents never would let go, or the inconsolable grief at the death of a husband.

On the other hand, there is in the New Testament a certain incongruous light-heartedness even in the face of tragedy which can be accounted for in no other way. For instance, at one point Paul goes so far as to say that it really makes very little difference whether he lives or dies: "For to me to live in Christ and to die is gain" and "whether we live or die we are the Lord's." On the bare face of it this sounds almost irresponsible, a giving in to a kind of fatalistic meaninglessness: "It doesn't matter really whether I live or die." But it's not that, of course. Paul throws himself into his work as an apostle with unlimited fire and enthusiasm as if everything depended on it. He knows full well what it means to live dangerously and purposefully. It simply is an indication of the lighthearted attitude, or perhaps "light-fingered" is the better phrase, a kind of openhanded attitude toward life here on earth; the "light-fingered" attitude which is possible when a man acknowledges that he *is* a stranger and pilgrim. Death holds no terrors, and life consequently is not to be squeezed by the throat until it surrenders itself to our appetite for a false and spurious security.

Thus a man of faith, who acknowledges that he is a stranger and pilgrim whose ultimate citizenship, as Paul puts it, is "in heaven," is free to give himself to the baffling and monumental problems of life in this world as a concerned citizen of his country in a way that the man who tries to make himself believe that this earth holds the only life-home there is cannot do. The man of faith is *free* from the fundamental anxieties and frustrations of his own existence to give himself in love to others. For no man is free to love until and unless he is freed from an overweening concern for his own future and destiny.

Moreover, the man of faith recognizes that he cannot possibly "build the kingdom of God" here on earth since obviously the kingdom is God's doing, not ours. The evil in the world and in ourselves cannot possibly be handled by sheer will power, intelligence, and good will alone. The poison in us runs too deep. In short, we cannot transform an inn into a permanent home no matter how hard we try or how impeccable we believe our motives to be. But if we know where our true home is, then we can, as Paul puts it, significantly enough at the close of that magnificent passage on the resurrection, "be steadfast, immovable, always abounding in the work of the Lord, knowing that our labor is not in vain in the Lord."

Only as we acknowledge, as men of faith, that we are strangers and pilgrims on this earth can we ever arrive at the place where, as Paul puts it, "we are no longer strangers and exiles but fellow citizens with the saints and members of the household of God."

But is Paul saying that here in a community on earth we have at last found our true home? "No longer strangers and exiles but fellow citizens with the saints and members of the household of God?" Every self-conscious Christian community is tempted to think so.

But the community of love, the visible expression of the church here on earth, even when it comes closest to being its true self, is not our ultimate home. For if we think of it so, we try to grasp it with both hands and squeeze a sense of community out of it. Doubtless our constant preoccupation with the attempt to realize a sense of community in a parish or to create community through the small group movement within a parish is due in part to the temptation to believe that here, at least, we can escape the fact that we are strangers and pilgrims—travelers of the Way. But we can't. The Christian community on earth can never be more than the barest hint of what lies in store. The only possible way to be at home in a Christian community is to recognize that this is not our permanent home either. Here too, as in the family, we have to learn to receive it with an open hand, not with fingers clutched to grasp and to hold. Here too we are strangers and pilgrims, as was Paul in the midst of the community of love back there in the first century. No longer strangers and exiles with respect to God at the center, we are members of the household of God, to be sure, but still strangers and pilgrims, passing travelers of the Way.

It all comes down in the end to this apparent contradiction: Only as we come to know that this earth is not our true home can we ever find ourselves truly at home here. And it is out of this apparent contradiction, this tension, that the life of the Christian grows and develops: no longer the aching homesickness or the frantic efforts to transform an inn into a permanent residence. The estrangement and sense of exile are transferred from the center of life to the peripheral and the passing. A man is at home in this lovely, fascinating, and often tragic world because he knows where his true home lies. "These all died in faith, not having received what was promised, but having seen it and greeted it from afar, and having acknowledged that they were strangers and exiles on the earth. For people who speak thus make it clear that they are seeking a homeland. . . . "Therefore God is not ashamed to be called their God, for he has prepared for them a city."

INDEX

Names and Subjects

INDEX

List of Preaching Texts

Type, 11 on 13 and 10 on 11 Garamond
Display, Lydian
Paper, White "R" Antique